Interpreting and Negotiating Licensing Agreements

A GUIDEBOOK FOR THE LIBRARY, RESEARCH, AND TEACHING PROFESSIONS

Arlene Bielefield and Lawrence Cheeseman

Neal-Schuman Publishers, Inc.
New York   London

Published by Neal-Schuman Publishers, Inc.
100 Varick Street
New York, NY 10013

Printed and bound in the United States of America

Library of Congress Cataloging-in-Publication Data

Bielefield, Arlene.
    Interpreting and negotiating licensing agreements : a guidebook for the library, research, and teaching professions / Arlene Bielefield, Lawrence Cheeseman.
        p. cm.
    Includes index.
    ISBN 1-55570-324-0
    1. License agreements—United States—Popular works.
2. Librarians—United States—Handbooks, manuals, etc. 3. Teachers—United States—Handbooks, manuals, etc. I. Cheeseman, Lawrence.
II. Title.
KF2980.B54   1999
346.7304'8—dc21   98-55929
                                                                      CIP

Contents

Preface   vii

Part I Understanding Licensing Agreements

1 What Is a Licensing Agreement?   3
   Licenses Are Contracts   3
   Parties to a Contract   5
      Corporations and Contracts   5
      Municipalities and Counties   6
      States and Contracts   7
   Contracts May Be Oral or Written   7
      Oral Contracts   7
      Written Contracts   9
         Licenses as Written Contracts   10
   Discharge of a Contract   11
   Breach of Contract   13
      Remedies for Breach of Contract   13
      Defenses to Actions for Breach of Contract   14

2 The Growing Use of Licensing Agreements   17
   Shrink-Wrap Licenses   17
      Implications of Shrink-Wrap Licenses
         for Schools and Libraries   21
   Webwrap Licenses   22
   Negotiated Licenses   23
   Why Is Licensing So Prevalent?   24
   Notes   27

3   What Do Licensing Agreements Really Mean?   29
        Clauses That Appear Frequently
            Parties   32
            Definitions   33
            Grant   35
            Licensor Obligations   37
            Term   39
            Renewal   42
                Automatic Renewal   43
                Non-Automatic Renewal   44
            Term and Renewal   45
            Fees   47
            Conditions of Use or Scope of License   51
            Authorized Users   54
            Limitation of Liability or Disclaimer   56
            Termination   58
            Governing Law   60
            Alternative Dispute Resolution   62
            Complete Agreement   65
            Support or Documentation   66
            Assignment   68
            Waiver   69
            Severability   70
            Confidentiality   71
        Clauses That Appear Less Frequently   72
            Content and Copyright   73
            Monitoring Use   74
            Privacy Protection   76
            Indemnification or Hold Harmless   77
            Government Use   78
            Amendments   79
            Force Majeure   80
            Signature Authority   81

Part II Making Decisions about and Negotiating Licensing Agreements

4 Copyright or Licensing Agreement?   85
School, Library, and Researcher Rights
under Copyright Law   86
Facts and Ideas Exception   86
First Sale Doctrine   88
Fair Use   91
Special Rights Granted to Libraries and
Archives   93
Digital Millennium Copyright Act of 1998   93
Making the Decision   94
Notes   94

5 Negotiating the License   99
Are All Licenses Negotiable?   99
The Negotiation Process   100
Will a Licensor Always Negotiate Terms
and Conditions?   102
How to Negotiate As a Potential Licensee   102
Banding Together—A Better Way to Go?   105

Appendixes
A Checklist for Evaluating Licenses   107
B Digital Millennium Copyright Act of 1998:
Provisions Relating to Libraries and Archives   113
C International Coalition of Library Consortia
Statement of Current Perspective and Pre-
ferred Practices for the Selection and Purchase
of Electronic Information   119

Glossary: Licensing Agreements A-Z   137
Notes   152
Index   155

Preface

It almost impossible to use—much less to buy or to subscribe to—any type of electronic media today without being asked to agree to complex legal terms governing your (or your students' or yours users') use of that product. As librarians, researchers, or educators we are finding ourselves increasingly (and usually involuntarily) immersed in reading and trying to abide by terms and phrases few non-legal professionals understand.

We are confronted with yet another license almost every time we use a commercial electronic product or service for the first time. When we open a new software program, we find a shrink-wrap license; when we sign up with a new Internet Service Provider (ISP) or sign up for a free news or financial service on the Web, a Webwrap or click-wrap license (one of those strange boxes on which you must click on "Yes" or "I Agree" before you can proceed) shows up on our screen; and many of us deal regularly with more formal licenses we must sign before we or our users can access electronic sources such as CD-ROM encyclopedias or databases. Most licenses seem impenetrable, many use terminology that seems hopeless or just plain wrong, and almost all absolve their producers of almost any responsibility if their use causes harm to your institution's network or computers.

Regardless of whether you can understand their incomprehensible language (or even read their small print), licenses *are* contracts. When we agree to a license's terms—whether that agreement is indicated with a notarized signature or a click on the "I agree" box on a Web site—we enter into a legally binding contract. While a professional (ideally an attorney with experience in contracts) needs to look at the implications any license holds for an institution like a school system or a library, it is now imperative that those of us who regularly deal with licensing agreements: (1) understand their intent and their terminology, (2) realize that licenses can be adjusted or amended, and (3) recognize the red flags they sometimes contain.

It is with these three goals in mind that we wrote *Interpreting and Negotiating Licensing Agreements*. Our primary audience is librarians, researchers, and teachers who need to understand these agreements so that they can purchase and subscribe to electronic resources with confidence. We want our readers to be able to act as good stewards of their institutional resources and not incur unnecessary liabilities— or sign away privileges accorded to them by a new copyright law Congress passed in 1998. Our secondary audience is those who draft and negotiate licensing agreements for these professions (such as software producers, Web site creators, and those who sell electronic products).

Interpreting and Negotiating Licensing Agreements is intended to be an easy-to-follow guide through the licensing maze with particular emphasis on school, library, and university needs. It is arranged to serve as both a comprehensive guide to working with licensing agreements and as a quick reference resource. Institutions such as schools and libraries not only have special needs, they also have special privileges. Librarians and other information professionals need to be aware of these privileges and know how to ensure that their users' legal rights are respected in the agreements into which they enter. We hope that if you use *Interpreting and Negotiating Licensing Agreements* as you wade through two or three licensing agreements, your vocabulary will expand, your comfort level with complex licenses will grow, and your ability to protect your institution will vastly increase.

Your attorney can then serve as your second pair of eyes, rather than as your personal guide through every clause.

Interpreting and Negotiating Licensing Agreements' five chapters explain the how and the what of licenses. These five chapters are followed by three appendices and a glossary—tools to help alleviate the stress and time-consuming aspect of negotiating a license.

Chapter 1 is titled simply "What Is a Licensing Agreement?" Because a licensing agreement is actually a contract, Chapter 1 is designed to be a layperson's introduction to contract law.

Chapter 2, "The Growing Use of Licensing Agreements," identifies and describes the various types of licensing agreements: shrink-wrap, Webwrap, and custom licenses that are negotiated clause-by-clause. Examples are used to illustrate common uses of these types of licenses and their ramifications for schools and libraries.

Chapter 3, "What Do Licensing Agreements Really Mean?" features a clause-by-clause examination of licenses. An easy-to-use chart offers one or more examples of each clause, explains what it means, and tells the reader what cautions should be exercised in interpreting it. Language that librarians and other educators should resist accepting (and in some cases, that they should never agree to) is noted in the commentary.

Chapter 4, "Copyright or Licensing Agreement?" is designed to help you protect yourself from unwittingly signing away special rights accorded to your institution under copyright law. It will help you ask and answer crucial questions such as: Is the material available somewhere else in an unlicensed form? (Because if it is, you may not need to enter into a restrictive licensing agreement.) What rights or alternatives do your users have before accepting the terms of the license? What special rights do schools, libraries, and researchers have under copyright law? And, perhaps most importantly, which are better for you to exercise: those special privileges accorded to libraries, schools, and researchers under copyright law or the terms of the license under consideration?

Chapter 5, "Negotiating the License," helps you determine which licenses are likely to be negotiable and which are not. We describe the negotiating process and suggest ways to use it effectively. We also tell why librarians should *never* agree to one increasingly common clause because it can undermine the very mission of libraries.

Appendix A, "Checklist for Evaluating Licenses," is a ready-to-copy tool to help you examine a license clause-by-clause. The checklist also suggests alternative clauses or phrases to replace unnecessarily restrictive language and suggests rights (such as appropriate definitions of authorized users or interlibrary loan privileges) you might want included in licenses.

Appendix B is the text of the Digital Millennium Copyright Act of 1998: Provisions Relating to Libraries and Archives. This new legislation give librarians, researchers, and educators special rights (which we also discuss in Chapter 3). We included the full text of the provisions relating to libraries and archives in this book so that you could have it at hand as you read licenses and negotiate terms.

Appendix C contains the full text of the International Coalition of Library Consortia's (ICOLC) "Statement of Current Perspective and Preferred Practices for the Selection and Purchase of Electronic Information." Many of this statement's tenets will be useful as you talk to producers and publishers about license terms.

Finally, we've included a glossary that explains contract terms in simple English to help you wade through the mysterious and often arcane terminology in licenses.

Depending on their comfort level with licensing, some people who pick this book up may want to read it from cover to cover; others may wish to use it as a reference work, concentrating on the chart of clauses, the glossary, and the checklist. However *Interpreting and Negotiating Licensing Agreements* is used, our hope is that licensing agreements no longer seem impenetrable and that librarians, educators, and researchers will never be intimidated into agreeing to onerous conditions. Our goal throughout this guide is to help librarians and educators interpret and negotiate licenses successfully and with confidence.

Arlene Bielefield, J.D., M.L.S.
Lawrence Cheeseman, M.L.S.

Part I
Understanding Licensing Agreements

1
What Is a Licensing Agreement?

- *Are licensing agreements governed by state law or by federal law?*
- *Under what conditions would a contract signed by both parties be voidable or unenforceable?*
- *What special concerns apply to contracts executed by municipally governed libraries?*
- *Are the licenses contained in packages of software really contracts?*
- *When is a contract ended?*

LICENSES ARE CONTRACTS

A licensing agreement (or simply, a license) is a contract. A contract is a legal agreement between two or more people, agencies, companies, institutions, or other entities (called *parties to the contract*) that involves an exchange of mutual promises to do something. (For example, one party might agree to provide access to a particular database and the other party might agree to use that database under certain conditions and to pay for the service.) A contract may be enforceable, voidable, or unenforceable; oral or written; express or implied; unilateral or bilateral. Some contracts span more than one of these categories (which are all discussed in this chapter).

In order to understand licensing agreements one must first become familiar with the basics of contract law. Contract law is state law. However, to facilitate commerce, the states have all adopted some form of the Uniform Commercial Code. Thus there are basic terms and conditions that have the same meaning across the country. But there are also differences—particularly in how state courts interpret the law. This chapter explains these national common meanings and aspects of the law.

The most basic contract consists of three parts—an offer, an acceptance, and consideration. An accepted offer becomes a promise for which consideration is rendered. Consideration may be money or some other inducement, such as statements of endorsement, for fulfilling the contract.

Contracts that the courts recognize as valid are called *enforceable* contracts. Should a party to an enforceable contract fail to fulfill its part of the bargain, the courts provide legal remedies to redress the injured party. To be enforceable, a contract must include five elements:

- legally competent parties
- mutual agreement by these parties
- consideration
- an agreed-upon time frame for completion of performance
- the required document format, if any, as stated in the state law of jurisdiction

Even when a contract is agreed to by both parties, is in writing, and is signed and dated, it may be *voidable* (cancellable). For example, if one of the parties is incompetent or if fraud is used by one party to induce the other party to contract, there is a voidable contract. However, such a contract is not automatically void. The contract will stand unless an aggrieved party makes a request that the contract be voided by a court.

A contract may also be *unenforceable*. One example of an unenforceable contract is an oral contract made for the purchase of a piece of land. Contracts for the purchase of land must be in writing. Therefore, the oral contract is unenforceable.

An example involving schools or libraries with an unenforceable license could occur if a vendor goes bankrupt, fails to supply the agreed-upon product, and is unable to repay fees the school or library paid the vendor in advance to attain the best discount.

PARTIES TO A CONTRACT

The parties to a contract, whether persons or institutions, are those making the offer (*offeror*[s]) and those accepting the offer (*offeree*[s]). For example, Microsoft is the offeror of Windows 98 and the library obtaining that product is the offeree.

For a contract to be legally enforceable, any contracting persons must be legally competent—they must be of a legal age for consenting to a contract and they must have both the capacity and the authority to contract. In a typical public library licensing situation, the library board designates an agent to sign or accept legal documents, such as licenses. That person may or may not be the library director. In a school system, the school board appoints an agent for such duty, usually the superintendent of schools.

Corporations and Contracts

To enter into a contract, a corporation must be empowered to enter into such agreements—that is, it must have the legal capacity to contract. This power to contract is generally set forth in the articles of incorporation and the charter of a company. If a company contracts to do something that is not empowered by its articles of incorporation or its charter, then it is acting outside its powers (*ultra vires* is the legal term). A corporation acting outside its powers is the equivalent of an individual who is incompetent to make a contract. *Ultra vires* contracts and those made by incompetent persons are voidable at the option of the incompetent party. Such contracts may also be judged unenforceable by the courts.

What types of libraries fit into the corporate mold? Those in for-profit businesses, of course. But, private colleges and universities are also corporate entities. Library consortia are usually nonprofit corporations. The legal status of school systems varies from state to state, but, in general, school systems are either viewed as state or local entities—sometimes both—rather than as private corporations.

The organizational scheme for public libraries varies widely across the United States. In some states, "association libraries" that are independent, nonprofit corporations provide public library service to a local populace. These libraries often receive some or most of their operating money from the municipality that they serve, yet their legal status is that of an independent entity.

For libraries in any of these corporations, it is essential to know who has the legal capacity to contract, so that licenses are agreed to by that authority.

Municipalities and Counties

Those who work for municipalities or counties (which are entities set up under state law) should be aware that strict rules are usually in effect concerning entering into contracts, with specific procedures that must be followed. These rules and procedures deal with how a contract is approved and who has the authority to agree to a contract. Often, municipalities require a bidding process to determine who will be awarded a contract. A library vendor may be selected through such a process, with the requirement that the library obtain all resources through the selected vendor. The bidding process may possibly be waived, however, when a product is available only from one source.

Public libraries that are town or county departments are subject to the parent governmental unit's rules of contracting. Some of these libraries have boards of trustees or directors and others do not. The town or county may delegate the contracting role to the library board or may require that the library adhere to the same process as other town or county departments that lack boards.

Because licensing library resources is a relatively new experience for libraries in towns and counties, a review of the proper procedure for licensing library resources is essential.

States and Contracts

A variety of libraries exist under a state's umbrella. These may include state libraries, legislative libraries, prison libraries, and state college and university libraries, as well as libraries in other types of state institutions. State laws require certain checks and balances for the expenditure of any funds. A bidding requirement is common at the state level, again with an exception for sole-source items. The ability to okay a license or to sign a contract tends to be designated to someone at a high level of authority in the state—for example, the state librarian usually is the only person in the library who can give the go-ahead on a license.

Because of these checks and balances, it may be difficult for state agency libraries to negotiate licenses or prices for electronic resources through traditional library consortia. On the other hand, libraries in a variety of one state's institutions can form their own consortia and, because of their considerable buying power, negotiate favorable terms and fees.

CONTRACTS MAY BE ORAL OR WRITTEN

Both oral and written contracts may create legally binding obligations that the courts find enforceable.

Oral Contracts

An everyday example of an oral contract is a school librarian who looked through a supply catalog, found something she needed, called the supplier and placed an order with a customer or purchase order number, was given an invoice number, received the material with an invoice, and authorized payment of the invoice through the school business office. The supplier offered goods through the catalog, the librarian accepted that offer through her telephone order, and the payment constituted consideration. No formal written contract was needed, but each party relied on the other for performance of a part of the contract. This kind of oral contract would be considered an *express contract*, since the terms were agreed to by the parties—the librarian agreed to the price as stated in the catalog, the supplier agreed to deliver the goods and to invoice the school system.

An oral agreement may constitute an *implied contract*, rather than an express contract. An example of an implied (or implied in fact) contract is a person who went into a restaurant, sat down, studied the menu, ordered a meal, ate the meal, and paid the bill. Without a formal agreement and with only oral communication between the parties, each party relied on the other to fulfill a part of the bargain—the customer expected a meal as described on the menu, the restaurant saw an implied promise for payment. Note that in this situation there was no formal step—such as a purchase order number—given to the server. The customer was not questioned regarding method of payment prior to serving the food, as in the previous example. In fact, in this case the contract was entered into and performed in a very short time.

Oral contracts can be difficult to enforce. Each side in a dispute about an oral contract has a different version of what went wrong and why. Each party may believe what he or she says is true even though the stories coming from the two parties are contradictory. The court must be persuaded as to whose version of what happened is correct. (For example, in each of the cases above, if something went wrong—if the school librarian refused to authorize payment because she claimed never to have placed that order or if the person who ordered the food stood up and left without touching any of it—there would surely be two versions of what happened and why.) While oral contracts exist and may be tempting, they have no place in the library licensing arena.

Written Contracts

Because of the difficulties involved in settling disputes surrounding oral contracts, the Statute of Frauds was developed in 1677 in England. The Statute of Frauds requires that certain types of contracts be in writing. In the United States, almost all states have adopted or adapted sections of the Statue of Frauds. These state laws tend to vary significantly, with each jurisdiction tailoring the law to its needs.

Examples of contracts that state laws commonly require be in writing include:

- a contract not expected to be completed within a year
- a special promise to answer for the debt, default, or miscarriage of another person
- a contract made upon consideration of marriage, other than a mutual promise to marry
- a lease for longer than a year
- the sale of real property or an interest in such property
- the authorization or employment of an agent on commission to purchase or sell real estate or lease such for more than a year
- a mortgage agreement
- an agreement that by its terms is not to be performed during the lifetime of the promisor

The Uniform Commercial Code (UCC) also determines whether contracts must be written. Developed by the National Conference of Commissioners on Uniform State Laws and the American Law Institute, the UCC deals with most aspects of commercial transactions. Contracts for the sale of goods over $500, those for the sale of securities, and certain contracts involving personal property require written agreements under the UCC.

States tend to add classifications of agreements (such as sales warranties, vehicle repair contracts, and loan agreements) to those that must be in writing in their jurisdictions. This is frequently in response to consumer complaints or proposed amendments to the Uniform Commercial Code.

Presently, licensing agreements are not covered under the UCC, although work is being done to establish Article 2B to deal specifically with licenses. For specifics on this issue, please see Chapter 2.

Licenses As Written Contracts
In general, although oral contracts may be enforced, written contracts are preferable. In the world of licensing, written agreements are the norm—a standard industry practice whether or not a particular state's law speaks to the issue. This development is the result of the need for the producers of electronic resources to protect their investments and copyrights.

Written licenses, and other types of contracts, are sometimes *unilateral* and sometimes *bilateral.*

An example of a unilateral licensing agreement is the type called a shrink-wrap license or an end user license agreement (eula). A shrink-wrap license can be found tucked in the package of a piece of computer software. In that shrink-wrap license the software provider states the terms and conditions of use and tells the user that acceptance of these terms and conditions will be demonstrated by the installation of the software onto the user's computer. The elements of a contract are all there:

- The software provider (offeror) offers a product with certain terms and conditions.
- The client (offeree) accepts that offer by loading the software onto the computer.
- The price paid for the software is the consideration

Those who wonder if shrink-wrap contracts are enforceable (because a contract in their minds is a signed agreement) should know that some courts have found such contracts, or licenses, to be invalid while others have found them to be enforceable. Further discussion of shrink-wrap licenses and examples of the court decisions are found in Chapter 2.

A bilateral contract is a written agreement that is negotiated and signed by both parties. Some licenses fall into this category. A library consortium might approach a producer or vendor of an electronic database and negotiate a license that is not the standard one offered by the licensor. Some of the original license clauses remain the same while changes to others are negotiated to satisfy the needs of the member libraries. (For example, the initial license presented for a magazine index might be rejected because the libraries view licensor requirements for information about the users and uses as an invasion of users' privacy.) Counterproposals may flow back and forth until clauses acceptable to both parties are developed.

It is important to note here that negotiation may take place at any point in the process of making the contract. For further discussion of negotiation, see Chapter 5.

DISCHARGE OF A CONTRACT

Contracts may be ended (*discharged*) in a number of ways. The most common one is full performance—that is when both parties fulfill their parts of the bargain within the specified time period.

But there are also possibilities for discharge before completion of the contract or license, and each has numerous variations and complications. The following descriptions of a few alternative ways to end a contract offer only the most uncomplicated circumstance in each instance.

- *Rescission*—In a situation where no third party is affected, it may be possible for the two parties to mutually agree to rescind a contract, particularly before performance has begun. One example is a case where the library's budget has suffered an unexpected cut, making the acquisition of the electronic resource in question impossible at the moment (the license having just been agreed to and signed). While the licensor could insist, that would be bad customer relations. Both sides are hopeful that restoration of funds will occur and that the license may be reinstated. However, there is agreement at the moment to rescind, since payment has not been made and installation has not yet taken place.

- *Substitute contract*—The parties may agree to a different performance or performer for the promises involved in the original contract, resulting in a substitute contract which discharges the earlier one. For example, if a library's budget is increased more than anticipated, instead of the quarterly CD-ROM version of the index, the library could now afford the online version. A substitute license might be developed and put in place, discharging the earlier one.

- *Accord and satisfaction*—The parties may agree that the offeror will substitute a different product or service from the one originally contracted for (*accord*) and that substitute may be made and accepted (*satisfaction*). For example, a school library that contracted for the third edition of an encyclopedia might be offered the fourth edition (which came out earlier than expected) under the same terms and conditions.

- *Novation*—With the mutual agreement of all the parties, one of the original parties to the contract might remove himself or herself from the contract and be replaced by a newcomer. Consider, for example, the Midville College Library which has licensed the Medical Journal. The Midville Medical College, a major new college division, is about to open its own library. There is agreement with the Medical Journal that the Midville Medical College Library will become the licensee, replacing the Midville College Library.

- *Account stated*—In a situation where one party receives an itemized statement of products purchased and billed for, or of expenditures made on the party's behalf (for example, a monthly bank statement), the party receiving the statement must question or object to disputed items within a reasonable time or the statement will be held to be enforceable. This is also true if an account is believed to have been appropriately discharged. For example, consider the school library that had a license for Internet service from the Netnet provider. After a year of that service, the library decided to migrate to another provider. The school library believed that Netnet was notified of the cancellation. However, a year after the so-called cancellation, a school business office report revealed that Netnet had continued to bill the school and the school had paid. No one knows how the mix-up occurred. Recoupment of the fees will depend on the good will of Netnet or, alternatively, on whether a court looks upon the questioning of the charges as occurring within a reasonable time.

- *Bankruptcy*—A petition for bankruptcy allows the discharge of a contract entered into by the petitioner. This unusual, but clear-cut, situation could arise when a library or school licenses an electronic product from a company that subsequently declares bankruptcy.

BREACH OF CONTRACT

Breach of contract is the failure to meet the terms of the contract in a timely fashion. The breach may be partial or total. For example, if the library budget suffers unexpected cuts and the library fails to pay the license fees, that is a breach of contract. Or, if the licensor installs software but it simply does not work, and months go by with no improvement, that is a breach of contract.

Remedies for Breach of Contract

The courts provide protection for the parties involved by establishing remedies for the failure of a party to carry out his or her part of the bargain. The remedies for breach of contract are based on the effort to put the offended party in the same position as if the contract had been fully performed.

In some instances, the remedy sought may be *specific performance*. This remedy is most often sought where a one-of-a-kind service or item is at issue. Suppose, for example, that a library struck a deal with a furniture dealer for a set of old cabinets that fit uniquely into a space in the reading room. When the cabinets were not delivered on the agreed-upon day, inquiries revealed that the dealer had subsequently had a higher offer and had delivered the cabinets to the higher-paying customer. An action for specific performance (i.e., delivery of the cabinets) might be the remedy sought, since no other cabinets fit into the decor of the library and into that particular space.

An example involving a license is a college library that licenses a new e-journal about neuroscience yet no issues are forthcoming halfway through the school year. Other journals are available on the same topic but they are more expensive. The court might mandate that the licensor cancel the license and give a refund as a remedy, or, alternatively, the court might direct the equivalent of specific performance through the provision of a substitute journal at the licensor's expense.

Another type of remedy is an award of money damages. However, to receive money damages there must be evidence of financial loss. Although evidence of financial loss is rare, it could happen. For example, consider the school system that negotiated a license for an online information service that is an integral component of a reading improvement program. The school has won a $40,000 federal grant to fund the program. Two months into the program, the licensor of the information service has failed to furnish the agreed-upon service. The granting agency has just paid an inspection visit and is threatening to take back the grant money. If it does, based on the licensor's failure to perform, the court might be persuaded to award money damages for the financial loss.

Defenses to Actions for Breach of Contract

To bring an action for breach of contract, the statute of limitations must be observed. Each state sets its own statute of limitations (the time period allowed for bringing a complaint), so state law must be examined to determine whether a breach action is timely.

Mental capacity, duress, misrepresentation, or mistake may be raised as defenses, particularly in regard to the party's assent to the contract. If assent to the contract was by a person who was incompetent, under duress, or the victim of either misrepresentation or mistake, then the contract may be either voidable or unenforceable.

A claim of illegality, if proven, is a successful defense to a breach of contract action. An inability to perform because of some outside force—such as an ice storm that knocks out the power lines in the licensor's city for three weeks—is also a viable defense.

Finally, failure of consideration, one of the essential elements of any contract, is a strong defense. Simply put, if payments are not made, for example, the licensor has a good defense for failure to provide the library with the electronic resource. Most licenses stipulate a payment schedule, which must be taken seriously.

While the general principles of contract law are in effect in all jurisdictions, the law of contracts, like other areas of the law, is ever-changing and has much untested ground. Contract law is state law, with the possibility for 50 different approaches to this important topic. The meaning and interpretation of words and phrases—even if a contract is written as required by law—can affect a licensing situation. The law under which a contract is developed may not be that of the library or school system's state.

The clauses of licenses (the boiler plate, or jargon, in particular) can seem very mysterious. The negotiation of licenses (contracts being purportedly negotiable instruments) for databases, electronic journals, and software is a new task for librarians, faculty, and researchers. Vendors and publishers, too, are entering this arena for the first time.

After this primer on contracts, it is now time to deal with licenses in detail as a specific genre of contracts.

2
The Growing Use of Licensing Agreements

- *What is a shrink-wrap license and is it enforceable?*
- *What about webwrap (or click-wrap) licenses?*
- *What is behind the exponential growth of licensing of electronic products?*

In this chapter, we look at each of the broad types of licenses, their characteristics, and their validity. We also examine the reasons why libraries, research institutions, and school systems have come to rely on licenses as the method of gaining access to electronic information resources.

There are three broad categories of licenses for electronic products:

- shrink-wrap licenses (also known as boxtop or tear-open licenses or **end user** license **agreements**, abbreviated eula)
- webwrap (or click-wrap) licenses
- negotiated-clause-by-clause licenses (hereinafter referred to simply as negotiated licenses)

A sample of clauses that may be found in any of these types of licenses is presented in Chapter 3.

SHRINK-WRAP LICENSES

The first link between electronic products and licenses seems to have occurred with the advent of the shrink-wrap license for computer software. While the majority of consumers, including schools and libraries, may think that they are buying software, they are not. They are only buying a limited ownership license to copy and use that software.

Shrink-wrap licenses are those fine-print documents that you find under the plastic wrap of software packages. You may or may not be able to read the document in its entirety before unwrapping the software. If the license can't be read from the outside of the package, there will be at least some indication of its existence on the outside of the package.

Opening the package is stipulated in the shrink-wrap license as an acceptance of the terms and conditions contained therein. The terms and conditions include limitations on liability of the licensor through warranty disclaimers as well as limits on possible damages. The shrink-wrap license generally spells out permissible uses of the software, including the limitation on making copies, a prohibition of simultaneous use on multiple computers, and the rights that accrue to the user who buys or is given the software in a transfer. There may be a reminder to the user that the copyright belongs to the licensor, and there is usually a prohibition on dissembling, reverse engineering, or decompilation. As with other types of licenses, shrink-wrap licenses have no standard format, so there may also be clauses limiting other matters.

Under the terms of the Computer Software Rental Amendments Act of 1989, libraries are able to loan software. The following warning statement *must* be affixed to the product:

> This computer program is protected under the copyright law. Making a copy of this program without permission of the copyright owner is prohibited. Anyone copying this program without permission of the copyright owner may be subject to payment of up to $100,000 damages, and, in some cases, imprisonment for up to one year.

The hallmark of the shrink-wrap license is that it is a unilateral contract; there is no good-faith bargaining of terms as there usually is in the world of contracts. Take it or leave it. Don't open the package if you don't like the terms (assuming you can read the terms and conditions without opening the package); just return it for a refund.

Even though people often don't read shrink-wrap licenses, failure to read the license is not an excuse to violate the terms. Or, at least one can't count on it being okay to violate the terms. The outcomes in shrink-wrap cases that have emerged from the courts are mixed. There are a limited number of cases in a limited number of jurisdictions, leaving most users to wonder about the outcome of a case to be brought in a state court on the issue of the enforceability of a shrink-wrap license. A statement of which state law governs the license may appear in a clause in the shrink-wrap license. On the other hand, there may be nothing on that topic, leaving the matter an interesting open question.

The few shrink-wrap license cases that have been filed have not been decided by state courts, because each included copyright questions, thus bringing them instead into the federal district courts and up on appeal to a federal circuit court. These cases include:

- *Vault Corp. v. Quaid Software, Ltd.* (1988)[1]
- *Step-Saver Data Systems, Inc. v. Wyse Technology and the Software Link, Inc.* (1991)[2]
- *Arizona Retail Systems, Inc. v. The Software Link, Inc.* (1993)[3]
- *ProCD, Inc. v. Zeidenberg* (1996)[4]

In the Vault case, Quaid Software sold software that prevented unauthorized software duplication. Vault obtained Quaid's software and then used reverse engineering to obtain Quaid's source code. Then Vault used a small portion of that code to generate his own program. Quaid's shrink-wrap license specifically prohibited reverse engineering. Quaid charged Vault with copyright infringement and breach of the shrink-wrap license. The case was brought in Louisiana where state law upheld shrink-wrap licenses, but the Fifth Circuit maintained that the U.S. Copyright Act preempted state law. The circuit court held that Vault's taking of a small part of the Quaid source code was a fair use. It further found that the shrink-wrap license was a contract of adhesion (not bargained in good faith—in fact, not bargained at all) and, therefore, invalid.

In the Step-Saver case, Step-Saver ordered software from The Software Link over the phone. Although the shrink-wrap license on The Software Link's software expressly disclaimed all warranties, Step-Saver had problems with the program and claimed a breach of warranty. The court found that a contract between the parties was formed at the time Step-Saver ordered the software via telephone. The court looked upon the shrink-wrap license as a modification of that contract, which under the UCC could only come about with the express agreement of both parties. Therefore, the court said, the shrink-wrap license was not binding on Step-Saver since there was no opportunity for agreement on the terms.

In Arizona Retail, Arizona Retail read The Software Link's shrink-wrap license, and after trying out the software, decided to keep it. When there were problems, Arizona Retail sued for breach of warranty. The court found that the shrink-wrap license, which disclaimed any warranty, was in effect since Arizona Retail had read it and used the software knowing about the warranty disclaimer clause.

In the ProCD case, Mathew Zeidenberg acquired ProCD's CD-ROMS with telephone numbers. These CD-ROMS came with shrink-wrap licenses which Zeidenberg read but decided to ignore. Zeidenberg took the information from the ProCD CD-ROMS and resold it via the Internet. ProCD raised a copyright question (are phone numbers copyrightable?), again bringing the case into federal court. In an earlier case (Feist, 1991),[5] phone numbers were found to be facts and copyright protection could not be claimed. Pro-CD wanted that question revisited.

ProCD also brought suit against Zeidenberg on violation of the license. The lower court (district court) found in favor of Zeidenberg because the shrink-wrap license had been inside the box, not outside where it could be read before opening the package. Thus the buyer could not ascertain all terms and conditions of the license before opening the package.

ProCD appealed. The Seventh Circuit Court of Appeals reversed the lower court, holding mass-market shrink-wrap licenses to be enforceable. In its decision, the circuit court found that the current UCC principles prevailed: that is, if the license terms are not objectionable, unreasonable, or unconscionable, then they are enforceable.

After the ProCD decision, the National Conference of Commissioners on Uniform State Laws and the American Law Institute, in developing a new article (Article 2B) for the Uniform Commercial Code (which is intended to deal with new technology), included the following statement in the draft of section 308:

> a party adopts the terms of a mass market license if the party agrees or manifests assent to the mass market license before or in connection with the initial use of or access to the information.[6]

The attempt to incorporate such language into the UCC as part of Article 2B has met with much criticism. It seems logical that if shrink-wrap licenses are recognized as valid to the extent that this new UCC article would seem to imply, they would, unlike the situation today, provide maximum protection for the licensor and could include clauses that would take away a number of rights presently held by licensees, including the privileges provided by the copyright law.

Implications of Shrink-Wrap Licenses for Schools and Libraries

Libraries, universities, school systems, and other publicly funded agencies and institutions may find that the take-it-or-leave-it aspect of a shrink-wrap license makes it impossible for the institution or agency to obtain the software to which such a license applies—state or local law sometimes prohibits these institutions from agreeing to certain clauses.

For example, publicly funded agencies and institutions are often prohibited from agreeing to fall under the jurisdiction of another state's laws. Therefore, if one of the clauses in a license states that disagreements arising out of the license will be settled under the laws of the vendor's home state, which is located halfway across the country from the licensee, then the publicly funded institution would need to look for a product not having this stipulation or one whose producer is willing to strike or modify that clause.

What will happen to shrink-wrap licenses? No one knows at this point. If the UCC revision comes to pass and the states adopt it, shrink-wrap licenses will assume new importance, and the courts will have reason to enforce them. If the UCC revision does not move forward, then the shrink-wrap's enforceability probably will remain to be determined by the courts on a case-by-case basis with varying outcomes. As this book goes to press, the UCC revision is still under consideration but has been slowed if not stopped by the outcries of a number of groups. Libraries and schools have cause for concern since the ramifications of the revision are not fully understood but may have the potential of limiting copyright privileges.

WEBWRAP LICENSES

What about webwrap (or click-wrap) licenses? These unilateral contracts appear on electronic resources and require the user to click "yes" to demonstrate acceptance of the licensing terms. How valid are these licenses?

Like shrink-wrap licenses, webwraps fail the good-faith bargaining test, but they are distinctly different from shrink-wraps. The primary difference lies in the fact that the potential licensee has every opportunity to read the webwrap. And, of course, there is the choice of "yes" or "no." It's still take it or leave it, but with a full opportunity to know what is being taken or left. With a shrink-wrap license, one may have accepted the terms and conditions before having the opportunity to read the whole license, just by opening the package. Not so with the webwraps.

Webwraps are easy to find on the Internet. For example, your Internet provider has one that you agreed to before using the service for the first time. Have you read it? If not, that's definitely something you should do. It's a great way to begin learning what clauses are common to licenses, what restrictions are put on use of the product, and what disclaimers the producer has made.

The fact that a webwrap license can be read in its entirety makes it more likely that a court will enforce it. The potential enforceability of the clauses of a webwrap license makes it vital that the person or persons who have the authority to agree to such a contract be fully informed about the meaning and the potential impact of each and every clause. Publicly funded institutions need to be especially careful. It can happen that a webwrap license, like a shrink-wrap license, may contain a clause or clauses that state or local laws forbid the library, university, school system, or other potential licensee from agreeing to—again, for example, the venue for dispute resolution. If the licensor is firm in maintaining the take-it-or-leave-it stance of the license as it appears online, then the potential licensee may need to find another product with acceptable licensing terms. If there is no other comparable product, it may be necessary to forgo a highly desirable product.

NEGOTIATED LICENSES

In theory, any license can be negotiated. However, in practice, certain licenses—shrink-wraps and webwraps in particular—are seldom negotiated. One reason that shrink-wrap licenses exist is that it would be almost impossible for the software companies that produce popular programs to contact and get agreement from every single purchaser. Given the dearth of cases on shrink-wrap issues, there is some reason to believe that the system in place is working well.

But, it is important to note that companies producing software for the mass market, with identical shrink-wrap licenses enclosed in each package to be purchased by individual buyers, commonly negotiate licenses clause by clause for use of that same software by a consortium or in an agency or institution with multiple workstations at one or several sites. In other words, circumstances dictate when bargaining will take place.

Negotiating a license is not nearly as cumbersome as it may seem at first contemplation. A number of clauses occur in almost every contract; other clauses may apply only to specific situations. A good many clauses are straightforward, easily understood, and acceptable to both sides; others may be the subject of lengthy discussion and of compromise. Ultimately, a negotiated license is reduced to paper, but it can be negotiated and transmitted back and forth electronically, by fax or e-mail.

WHY IS LICENSING SO PREVALENT?

As electronic resources of the kind used in public libraries, schools, and universities and colleges have proliferated, so have licenses for their use. Unlike books, videos, and audiocassettes, licensed electronic tools are not purchased outright.

Books, serials, videocassettes, and audiocassettes have been a part of the library, research, college and university, and school scene for a long time. People in academic settings are accustomed to being able to use these items freely (with copying being limited if allowed at all under the copyright law). Under the First Sale Doctrine of the copyright law, the owner of the physical object, while not owning the copyright, has the freedom to give away, sell, throw away, or keep the item.

Licensing a product makes it possible for the licensor to limit any use of that product, assuming that the licensee agrees to those limitations. The product owner controls the use. It is possible to agree to a license that strips the licensee of fair use and other privileges granted by the copyright law, for example. Licensees should be careful to look for such clauses and refuse to accept them. This is just one example of an extremely limiting clause that may appear in a proposed license agreement.

Publishers feel that they must exert control over the use of their electronic products. This desire for control is likely the reason for the exponential growth of licensing. Think about the ease of transmission of an electronic information source compared to a traditional resource. A piece of information can be electronically transmitted to any number of sites almost instantaneously. It is extremely easy to share material from an electronic source with those who have not subscribed to it, and there are no viable methods to monitor such sharing. Is it any wonder that producers of online databases, CD-ROMs and other electronic resources are nervous? How can they control this unruly universe? License the materials and make the licensee agree not to do certain things. Certainly, in the near future there will also be methods to monitor the use of licensed materials. For now, licensors must rely on the licenses to control use.

Are licensees always at a disadvantage? Of course not. With licensing, the marketplace controls. For example, if a licensor is the sole source of a popular product, the licensor is able to set more stringent terms than if the same or similar resources were offered by others. But bargaining power is the key to what a license allows and prohibits. That is why there is a trend in the library community, for example, to form consortia specifically for the purpose of negotiating group licenses. The buying power of a large group of libraries is sure to be influential in bargaining the terms of a license. That does not mean that a single library or other institution shouldn't attempt to change the terms of a license that the institution finds unacceptable. It just means that a single institution's ability to exert pressure on the licensor is not as great as that of a group.

While licensees are not always at a disadvantage, they are certainly encountering many new constraints on information use. For example, university libraries usually must assure a licensor that only the students, faculty, and administration of that university will have access to the licensed product—with a print resource, there was never a need to monitor what titles were being used by whom.

Among the common constraints that licensors seek to impose on licensees are limitations on lending, responsibility for damage by third-party users, copyright limitations, and surcharges for full-text materials. However, many publishers of electronic materials have shown a willingness to listen to the customer. The need for language that allows for interlibrary loans, for full copyright privileges, and for other issues of importance to licensees must be expressed to the licensor, who may not have any idea that such needs exist.

The licensing scene is ever changing. The content of electronic tools has changed substantially in a short time. Not long ago, an electronic index or abstract (often attained through a service such as Dialog) pointed the user to a print source. The terms of the license with such services were not negotiable. Today, the full-text materials themselves are available in electronic format directly from the publisher, and, more and more, licenses are negotiated.

In summary, licensing is a relatively new phenomenon in the library, research, and teaching fields. Thus people in these fields have a new set of skills to polish—including developing negotiating strengths and learning the vocabulary of licensing terms.

There is a balance in the marketplace—publishers of electronic content products need customers and customers need electronic products. This symbiosis is in itself a powerful reason for licensors and licensees to listen to each other and to strike a balance that benefits both parties.

NOTES

1. 847 F.2d 255 (1998).
2. 939 F.2d 91 (1991).
3. 831 F. Supp. 759 (1993).
4. 908 F. Supp. 640, rev'd 86 F.3d 1447 (1996).
5. 499 U.S. 340 (1991).
6. This proposed amendment to the Uniform Commercial Code has not yet been adopted.

3

What Do Licensing Agreements Really Mean?

- *Which clauses are the most frequently used in licensing agreements?*
- *What do they really mean?*
- *What cautions should always be used in interpreting them?*

Legal documents of any kind tend to intimidate the lay person. One reason is that lawyers have their own language, just as members of other professions do. Certainly, librarians, researchers, and teachers are as guilty of using jargon as lawyers. However, the law can have such a life-affecting role that people are at once in awe and in fear of it. Some of the language of contracts—including licenses—is as mysterious as other legal documents like deeds and wills. Added to all this is the fact that the vendor's (licensor's) counsel generates the license, and, in line with the counsel's responsibility, the license attempts to protect the rights of the vendor to the maximum while limiting the rights of the licensee.

Of course, some license clauses are simple to understand. Others, however, are incomprehensible to the lay person. Even when a clause in a license is readily understood, the effect that the clause could have may not be discerned easily.

The purpose of this chapter, then, is to point out what the common license clauses mean and also to point out some of the possible effects of the clauses. Samples of typical clauses (using a fictitious licensor, Zychon, that provides online almanacs) show some of the common language. Not all of the clauses presented in this chapter will appear in every contract, but some clauses will appear in almost every license. Sometimes more than one subject may be tucked into a clause, eliminating the necessity for a separate clause—for example, the term clause may also address renewal, thereby eliminating the need for a separate renewal clause.

There is, in fact, no standardized license format, which makes the job of putting together a primer on license clauses a bit more difficult. However, if a potential licensee is familiar with a broad range of possible clauses, he or she is in a much stronger position to avoid agreeing to onerous terms.

This chart provides examples and explanations of clauses that frequently appear in licensing agreements, and includes some cautions in interpreting them.

CLAUSES THAT APPEAR FREQUENTLY

There are clauses that appear in some form in most licences, and you need to be familiar with them to work effectively.

FREQUENT CLAUSES

1. Parties
2. Definitions
3. Grant
4. Licensor Obligations
5. Term
6. Renewal
7. Term and Renewal
8. Fees
9. Conditions of Use or Scope of License
10. Authorized Users
11. Limitation of Liability or Disclaimer
12. Termination
13. Governing Law
14. Alternative Dispute Resolution
15. Complete Agreement
16. Support or Documentation
17. Assignment
18. Waiver
19. Severability
20. Confidentiality

1. Parties

Clauses	Explanation	Cautions
Parties or Parties to the Agreement or Parties to the License.	The parties to the contract may be identified in a clause, usually the first clause in the contract.	Whether the information about the parties is in a separate clause or in a paragraph preceding the clauses in some other format, it is important that there be identification of the parties to the license.
or *Online Licensing Agreement*	or The identification of the parties may not be put into a clause, but may, instead, precede the license clauses. The license may start with a title on the top of the first page.	
Agreement made this ___ day of ___, 200__ by and between Zychon Publishing Co, Inc.("Licensor"), of Middletown, Colorado, USA, and ___ ("Licensee") concerning access to the Zychon online almanacs specified in Schedule A attached hereto and made a part hereof.	In a paragraph that precedes the clauses, there may be a statement identifying the parties.	

2. Definitions

After identification of the parties, a license may include a clause that contains definitions of important terms included in the body of the license.

Each definitions list is different in that it is tailored to the particular situation. It is possible, too, that the definitions are placed in a clause that does not appear at the beginning of the license. There are no rules about placement of this or any other clause.

2. Definitions

Clauses	Explanation	Cautions
"Agreement" includes the agreement itself and any appendices, schedules, or other addenda. *"Interlibrary loans" is the lending of licensed materials by one library to another library's user(s).* *"User" (see explanation)*	Particularly important to libraries, research facilities, and educational institutions is the definition of a "user." If user is not defined in a definitions section, there will usually be a license clause dealing with the subject.	When there is a definitions clause, it is important that all terms of substance in the license be defined with precision. Ask the question, for each of the defined terms, "Do I understand what this means? Is the meaning clear?" If not, do something about it. Otherwise, misunderstandings can occur and can lead to serious disputes.

3. Grant

When there is no definitions clause or if the definitions clause is placed later in the license, the first clause is often the grant clause.

3. Grant

Clauses	Explanation	Cautions
In consideration for the licensee's agreement to the terms and conditions herein, including payment of licensing fees as set forth in clause 5, Zychon, Inc., hereby grants to the licensee a nonexclusive, nontransferable right to access and use the almanacs in accordance with the terms and conditions set forth herein for the term of this agreement.	This clause states, in general terms, what the licensor is providing to the licensee.	There is an importance to this clause that its simplicity might disguise. It is in this clause that the vendor states what is being surrendered under this license. Because the "right to access and use" the vendor's products could conceivably mean different things to the parties to the contract, it is important that the terms and conditions be spelled out elsewhere in the contract to avoid misunderstandings and disagreements.

4. Licensor Obligations

Instead of the grant clause, there may be a licensor obligations clause. This clause tends to be more specific regarding what the licensor will furnish than a grant clause, which usually refers to an appendix or appendices for details.

4. Licensor Obligations

Clauses	Explanation	Cautions
Zychon shall establish one or more locations at which the almanacs will be available online for Authorized Users at Authorized Workstations. Except for those times when servers are down for maintenance or for loading data, Zychon will make a reasonable effort to make the almanacs accessible online continuously during the term of this Agreement.	This type of clause gives some specifics regarding what the licensee can expect from the licensor. Some licensor obligation clauses also include a statement about performance, stating that a reasonable effort will be made to have the system function as well as other similar systems.	This statement, of course, can be an empty promise, depending on what "reasonable effort" entails or what other systems are considered "similar."
Zychon cannot be responsible for downtime caused by failure of telecommunications lines or Internet nodes or servers.	This part of the clause that deals with downtime due to outside forces sometimes appears in a separate force majeure clause.	

5. Term

The term clause states how long the license runs and may state how the license can be renewed. In stating how long the license runs, the clause may refer to an attachment, schedule, or addendum. In general, the **term** or **term and renewal** clause is easily read and understood, even though there are numerous variations on the basic theme of a general statement of how long the license runs.

5. Term

Clauses	Explanation	Cautions
The term of this Agreement is for one year. or *The term of this Agreement is for one year beginning on July 1, 2002, and ending on June 30, 2003.* or *The term of this Agreement is for one year from the date of its signing by all parties. Should the dates vary, the latest date shall be the one from which the term commences.*	This clause might take several forms.	Succinct and to the point but perhaps too much so. When does the year start and when does it end? Succinct and to the point but with identification of the dates that the license encompasses. When the parties are not together to sign, this kind of approach might be useful.

5. Term (continued)

Clauses	Explanation	Cautions
The term of this Agreement is for the period set forth in Schedule A attached hereto and made part hereof.		Schedule A contains the information on how long the license is in effect. Such a schedule might contain very specific information such as the date the license begins, the date it ends, and possibly the beginning and ending hours on those dates. This format is used when a license is a standard one presented to all potential licensees, with any variations placed in schedules or addenda which are attached and made a part of the license.

6. Renewal

It is common for a license to mention renewal. If renewal comes about when the licensee does nothing, it is an *automatic* renewal. The automatic renewal clause usually has a provision whereby the licensee must notify the licensor within a stipulated time period. Because a licensee may have a variety of licenses coming up for renewal or cancellation at various times, this kind of clause can be a real nuisance. If the time period for cancellation slips by unnoticed, an automatic renewal goes into effect even if the licensee had an intention to cancel. The ideal is a clause providing for the licensor to signal the licensee at the beginning of each cancellation period for automatic renewal. However, usually the licensee bears the burden of staying alert to deadlines.

An automatic renewal clause may provide that the terms and conditions already in place, including pricing, stay the same with each renewal. However, the pricing clause or other provisions may make it possible for the price to change. Such changes are usually included in a schedule attached to the license.

If the licensee must do something to renew, renewal is *non-automatic*. Renewal clauses, whether automatic or not, may take a variety of forms. Some examples appear below.

A. Automatic Renewal

Clauses	Explanation	Cautions
This Agreement shall be automatically renewed for a year unless the licensor is notified in writing of nonrenewal by the licensee at least 45 [or some other agreed-upon number] days prior to the end of the current license term.	In this example, only the licensee can prevent renewal.	The automatic renewal clause written in this way stays in effect year after year, so the licensee must be ever alert to the timeframe that allows for cancellation.
This Agreement shall be renewed automatically for a year unless written cancellation notice is given by either party to the other at least 45 days prior to the end of the current license term.	This clause illustrates a more commonly found situation in that either party is given the right of cancellation with due notice. As with the previous example, the automatic renewal stays in effect from year to year if neither of the parties gives due notice to cancel.	For either example, payment schedule changes may be appended in a schedule made part of the contract, or there may be a clause opening the pricing issue after a certain number of automatic renewals.

B. Non-Automatic Renewal

Clauses	Explanation	Cautions
This Agreement may be renewed only with the written consent of all parties.	Here, whoever initiates the renewal process must obtain the agreement of the other party or parties.	

7. Term and Renewal

Some licenses incorporate the term and the renewal agreement into one clause. Again, in general, the term and renewal clause is easily read and understood.

7. Term and Renewal

Clauses	Explanation	Cautions
The term of this Agreement shall be for one year commencing on June 1, 2002, and ending on May 30, 2003, with automatic renewal for one year unless the licensor is notified in writing of an intention not to renew by the licensee at least 30 [or some other number of days as agreed] days prior to the end of the license term.	This clause incorporates into one clause the term of the agreement and an automatic renewal.	This combination can be a bane or a boon, depending on the situation. If the automatic renewal is at the same price as the first year of the license, perhaps that is a bargain. On the other hand, the fees clause, or an attached schedule, may contain an automatic increase for a second year. However, again the main problem with an automatic renewal clause is that, should the licensee want to terminate the contract, the notice of intention must be put in writing to the licensor at least 30 days (or some other time period) before the first license term expires.
The term of this Agreement shall be for a period set forth in Schedule B and made a part hereof and may be renewed only upon the written agreement of the parties [or of "both parties," if there are just two].	This clause incorporates into one clause the term of the agreement and a non-automatic renewal.	

8. Fees

While the fee clause is not the first one, it certainly is one of the most important clauses for both parties to the contract. Achieving a fair price is the goal of both the licensor(s) and the licensee(s). However, each party tends to have its own definition of "fair," which makes the negotiation of the fees clause complex. The licensee must determine how important the particular database or software is to the institution and its clients. Libraries, colleges and universities, and school systems must ascertain the importance of access to the information or other electronic material that the licensor is offering.

The pricing of information products in particular depends on how the licensed electronic product rates on the following factors:

- provides as much information or more than a print version
- is user friendly
- is as easy or easier to use than a similar product
- has unique features that make it essential or advantageous to the institution and its clientele
- requires the purchase or lease of new hardware or software, and, if so, what the costs are
- is of high quality
- can create savings for the licensee (through less need for storage, for example)
- requires an increase or decrease in staffing
- allows interlibrary loan privileges
- can be quickly installed
- has appropriate support from the licensor

In addition, the potential licensee must have some idea of volume of expected use, staff experience and training requirements, maintenance costs, conversion costs (if any), required user training, user preferences for electronic formats, and present and future pricing-structure possibilities. Other factors may be important in specific settings.

There seems to be no universally used measure or payment schedule in the licensing world. However, there are some common practices. Currently the major payment methods fall into four broad categories:

- monthly, quarterly, or annual subscriptions
- timed-access fees (pay by the minute or hour)
- per-search fees (pay per use)
- block-access fees (buy a period of time or a specified number of searches)

Fees (continued)

Method of Payment	Advantages and Disadvantages
1. Subscription	This payment method tends to be popular for several reasons: • It lets endusers—whether staff, researchers, students, or administrators—access the electronic product as long and as much as they wish, unless there is a simultaneous-user restriction. • The record-keeping for both a licensee and licensor is kept to a minimum under this method. • The licensee is in a position of knowing what to budget for the subscription, and the licensor has a guaranteed income.
2. Timed access	ADVANTAGE: common payment method. Per-minute or per-hour charges are familiar to people who have used such databases as Lexis/Nexis or Dialog. Often there is an initial charge and then a per-minute or per-hour rate based on whether the licensee is a nonprofit educational institution or a commercial entity. Timed-access payments are a feature of most Internet service provider who offer both limited-access and unlimited-access plans. DISADVANTAGES: unpredictable. Setting aside the dollars for timed-access searching requires an educated "guestimate." If it falls short in predicting actual use, either searching will have to be restricted or funds for more search time will have to be found. In other words, this payment method can have a large unpredictability component for both parties to the agreement.

Fees (continued)

Method of Payment	Advantages and Disadvantages
3. Per search	ADVANTAGE: licensee pays only for actual use.
	DISADVANTAGE: again unpredictable. Budgeting can be difficult. If the estimate of the number of searches—hence cost—is too low, searching may have to be restricted. Care must be taken, too, to clarify what constitutes a "search" before a licensee agrees to a per-search payment scheme for a license.
4. Block access	This approach to an electronic product is one way of controlling the amount of searching that takes place and the amount of money needed for access. Basically, the licensee sets up a deposit account with the licensor. A certain amount of money is paid to the licensor for an agreed-upon number of searches or a specified amount of search time (again, as with the per-search approach, the definition of a search must be clear). As the searches or the time are used, their price is deducted from the amount of dollars deposited. Further blocks may be purchased as needed. Block prices often include a discount from what a per-search method of payment would cost from the same vendor.

9. Conditions of Use or Scope of License

While the variations on this clause are endless, the example here serves as a basis for the examination of any such clause presented by a licensor to a licensee. The initial sentences shown in this example may appear in the grant clause in some instances.

9. Conditions of Use or Scope of License

Clauses	Explanation	Cautions
Zychon authorizes the licensee to provide on-site access to the online almanac to library patrons and staff. Information contained in the almanacs may be saved and/or printed for personal, noncommercial use by patrons providing that the copyright notices are preserved.	A general statement about the uses and users to which the licensee is entitled, this clause also includes the site restriction. Uses are generally limited to personal and noncommercial categories.	Although the language is simple, this clause contains vital information— including the basic rights and restrictions that apply to the licensor. The issues addressed are all of extreme importance. There must be good-faith bargaining on both sides for a fair and equitable balancing of rights.
To protect any proprietary material contained in the almanacs, the licensee is not allowed to alter, decompile, reverse engineer, disassemble, reverse assemble, or ascertain the source code.	This clause states the restrictions that pertain to the licensee in using the licensor's materials.	Some form of this clause will appear in most electronic resource licenses.

9. Conditions of Use or Scope of License (continued)

Clauses	Explanation	Cautions
Except as provided by this license, the licensee is not allowed to copy, modify, create derivative works, sub-license, rent, lease, donate, transfer, assign, or distribute the almanacs, or parts thereof, in other ways, including electronically.		
Schedule A contains the terms under which remote and other outside access is permitted.	If remote access is allowed, there is usually a reminder in this clause about the limitations on it—perhaps refering to an appendix or schedule	Many librarians have no need for remote access but those that do will generally find the topic in the scope of license clause.
The licensee will provide the necessary access lines, modem, telephone and computer equipment, and accessories needed to access the Zychon almanacs	The licensee's and licensor's responsibility regarding telecommunications equipment, hardware, and software may appear here as well.	This clause varies widely, depending on the circumstances of the parties. It is common for the library or school to provide hardware, telecommunications equipment, and the like.

10. Authorized Users

Clauses	Explanation	Cautions
The resources provided by the licensor are available for use by administrators, teachers, students, and staff affiliated with the Middleboro School system through the libraries located in the elementary, middle, and high schools. Remote access is available to the same users with authorized passwords. or *The licensor hereby grants to the licensee University—including its permanent, adjunct, and visiting faculty; its students; its administrators; and its employees—the right to access, retrieve, display, and make copies from the online form of the Zychon almanacs solely for their*	This kind of clause can take a number of formats. Here is an example.	All parties to the agreement have an interest in the identification of authorized users. Some of this interest lies in the fact that fees are often a function of the size of the user population. But serving the appropriate population and providing appropriate service are also important. If remote access is needed, it should be mentioned in this clause.

10. Authorized Users (continued)

Clauses	Explanation	Cautions
educational, scholarly, research, and personal use in accordance with the terms and limitations of this Agreement. Remote access is permitted with authorized passwords. or *The licensor hereby grants to the licensee libraries the right to provide access and permit copying from the Zychon online almanacs by members of the public for their educational, scholarly, research, and personal use by means of workstations located at the library facility and its branches, subject to the terms and limitations of this Agreement. Remote access to the online form of the almanacs by members of the public is [or is not] permitted.*		If remote access is needed, it should be mentioned in this clause.

11. Limitation of Liability or Disclaimer

Clauses	Explanation	Cautions
Zychon almanacs are licensed "as is" without warranty, express or implied, of any kind. Zychon disclaims all warranties, including but not limited to warranties as to quality, performance, or fitness of its almanacs for any particular purpose. Zychon does not make any warrant or guarantee regarding the accuracy or reliability of the electronic almanac. *Zychon shall not be liable for any direct, indirect, or consequential damages in connection with the use or performance of the almanacs. Zychon's liability shall in no event exceed the license fees paid under this Agreement.*	The licensor in the example has made no promise and, while disclaiming any liability, has at the same time noted a limitation of liability of no more than the fee paid—thus covering all the bases. This kind of clause is fairly common.	This clause is one that the licensee should read with great care, since it is the place where the licensor will deny any responsibility for errors or defects in the product being licensed. Perusing this example, which typifies such clauses, is the best way to understand why it is important for a potential licensee to be cognizant of the contents of these clauses. Know what you are getting. Some publicly funded institutions are forbidden from signing any kind of agreement that includes a limitation of liability such as that stated here, so it is important to have a university, college, school, or library attorney scrutinize the clause. If that kind of professional help is un-

11. Limitation of Liability or Disclaimer (continued)

Clauses	Explanation	Cautions
Zychon is not responsible for the content of any linked site on the World Wide Web accessed by the licensee and does not endorse any such site or imply that the information on the linked site is correct or accurate.		available, a private attorney with contract expertise is recommended, not only for this clause but also for others, such as the law under which disputes will be resolved.

12. Termination

Clauses	Explanation	Cautions
Multi-year Agreement: *Licensee or licensor may terminate this agreement upon written notice provided to the other party no later than 60 days prior to the close of any contract year as defined elsewhere in this agreement. Given such proper notice, licensor agrees to rebate fees for any contract year following the one in which either party elects to terminate this Agreement.* or *A. No refund or rebate of license fees shall be made for any portion of the term in which the licensee elects not to use the almanacs. In the event the term of this license is for a period greater than one year, licensee may terminate this agreement upon written notice provided to Zychon no ten notice provided to Zychon no*	Usually there is some way for each of the parties, with proper notice, to terminate the agreement. There are typically two parts to the notice requirement—that it be in writing and that it be given within a specified time. Clearly these are one-sided arrangements, in one case giving only the licensee cancellation rights and in the other the licensor. It is hard to imagine either party agreeing to such arrangements, but it can happen when the contract is not read carefully or is not fully understood	This example clause gives the same privileges and timeliness to both parties of the agreement. This is not always the case—something to watch for—as example 2 following demonstrates. Note that this clause refers to a calendar year rather than a contract year, a fact that could be easily overlooked. Libraries and schools might want the license for a school year or a fiscal year. Any phrase that indicates the contract term should be defined carefully, whether in a definitions clause or elsewhere.

12. Termination (continued)

Clauses	Explanation	Cautions
later than 60 days prior to the close of any calendar year. Zychon will rebate any fees paid for any calendar year following the one in which licensee elects to terminate this Agreement. *B. Zychon may terminate this Agreement for any or no reason upon 60 days written notice, in which case all previously paid fees representing unused portions of the term of this license shall be repaid to the licensee.* or *Either party may terminate this Agreement for any or no reason upon 60 days written notice and all previously paid fees representing unused portions of the term of this license shall be refunded to the licensee.*		In part B, the clause is not only one-sided but the licensor can cancel at any time with proper notice. Giving one party the privilege to cancel at any time while insisting that the other side have much more limited rights in this regard is not acceptable. Although this kind of clause is important should a need arise on either side to terminate the license, realistically the parties both have an interest in maintaining the license relationship. Thus terminations are rare.

13. Governing Law

Clauses	Explanation	Cautions
This Agreement shall be governed by the laws of the state of New York.	Contracts are governed by state law. When a license is generated, it is necessary to determine which state's law will govern that particular license. Often, the licensor will include a clause stating that the governing law will be that of the state in which the main offices of the licensor are located. The clause itself will be straightforward and simple	While the clause is straightforward, the implications of such a clause are not. Is New York the state of the licensor, the licensee, or neither? What does the law say about contracts? (License are, after all, contracts.) What are the advantages and disadvantages for the parties? Finding the answers to these questions may be complex, raising further questions. For a licensee, the law that is most familiar is that of the state in which the licensee resides. While there may be advantages in the law of another state, determining those advantages may not be an easy matter. In addition, if a dispute should arise, the licensee may not have the resources to hire professional help to bring a case or defend against one at a distance.

13. Governing Law (continued)

Clauses	Explanation	Cautions
		Further, some public institutions may be forbidden from agreeing to surrender to the laws of another jurisdiction. Many licensing agreements provide for alternative dispute resolution, however, in which case the governing law may have less importance than if there were no avenues for dispute resolution other than the courts. The importance of governing law can be weighed at the time that the governing law clause is being considered.

14. Alternative Dispute Resolution

Clauses	Explanation	Cautions
1. The parties to this Agreement shall make a good-faith effort among themselves to resolve any questions or settle any disputes concerning its interpretation. Unresolved questions or disputes shall be brought to arbitration under the commercial arbitration rules of the American Arbitration Association in effect at the time, with such arbitration being held in the city and state of the licensee.	To avoid the time and money involved in taking serious disagreements to court, contracts may have alternative dispute resolution pathways. These alternative methods include negotiation, mediation, and arbitration. Generally, it is in both parties' interests to settle matters at the earliest time and at the least cost in terms of time and money.	In this case, after a try at resolution of a question or dispute, the issue goes straight to an arbitrator. The issues that could be sticky include the time frame, which is unspecified here, and the selection process for the arbitrator. The time frame can extended because agreeing on an arbitrator can take time. In addition, once an arbitrator has been selected, that person's schedule will dictate when an arbitration hearing can take place.

If matters get to arbitration, that step usually involves considerable expense, since arbitrators are chosen through the American Arbitration Association. Arbitration may be binding or nonbinding. Nonbinding |

14. Alternative Dispute Resolution (continued)

Clauses	Cautions
2. The parties to this Agreement shall make a good-faith effort to resolve any questions or disputes that arise out of this Agreement—first through negotiation and then through mediation. Should those two methods of alternative dispute resolution fail to resolve the question or dispute, then the parties may agree to submit the problem to arbitration. These steps shall proceed as follows:	arbitration allows for further redress in the courts.
Negotiation A dispute arising between the parties during this Agreement will first be submitted in writing to a panel of two representatives, one selected by the licensor and one selected by the licensee. These representatives shall confer in a timely manner to resolve the dispute through good-faith negotiation. A resolution agreed to by the representatives shall be final and binding. If the representatives fail to negotiate a resolution to the dispute within fourteen (14) days after the submission to them, either party may request mediation in writing within ten (10) days after the failure of the negotiation.	To minimize time and money involved, some Alternative Dispute Resolution clauses contain a three-step process—negotiation, mediation, and arbitration. For those who prefer carefully structured processes, this kind of clause provides a predictable approach to disputes or questions about the agreement.
Mediation In the event of a failure of negotiation and upon the timely request of either party, the mediation process shall commence. The parties shall select a mutually acceptable mediator within fourteen (14) days after the date of the request for mediation. Neither party shall unreasonably withhold consent to the selection of a mediator. Each party	

14. Alternative Dispute Resolution (continued)

Clauses	Cautions
shall pay an equal share of the mediation costs. Upon a failure to resolve the dispute through mediation within fourteen (14) days after submission to the mediator, the dispute may be submitted to arbitration upon agreement by both parties within fourteen (14) days after the failure of mediation. Arbitration Any controversy or claim relating to this Agreement, if referred to arbitration, will be finally settled by compulsory arbitration in accordance with the Commercial Arbitration Rules of the American Arbitration Association (AAA). Either party may file the appropriate notice with the AAA. The arbitration proceeding will take place at the licensee's choice of location. An arbitration panel, consisting of three (3) arbitrators, one each chosen by the parties and one appointed by the AAA. The arbitrator's award will be the exclusive remedy of the parties for all issues submitted to arbitration. Each party will pay an equal portion of the costs of arbitration.	

15. Complete Agreement

Clauses	Explanation	Cautions
This Agreement with its attachments comprises the entire agreement between the parties with respect to its subject matter. Its supersedes any and all previous agreements oral or written between the parties. This Agreement cannot be amended or modified except in writing as agreed by the parties.	This clause is self-explanatory and is one of a number of variations that occur in licenses.	

16. Support or Documentation

Clauses	Explanation	Cautions
Licensee will receive telephone technical support from Zychon for the online almanacs 24 hours a day, 7 days a week, via a toll-free 800 line. or *Licensee will receive telephone technical support from Zychon for the online almanacs during regular business hours, Monday through Friday 8am–7pm, and Saturdays 10am–4pm.* or *Zychon provides several levels of support for its online almanacs:* *a. Electronic (e-mail) question answering service 24 hours a day, seven days a week*	An important part of the license agreement is the description, detailed or general, about the support that the licensee can expect from the licensor. There are a host of variations. Each party must determine what it can afford.	These sample clauses spell out the technical support available to a greater or lesser degree. Some licensors only promise to provide reasonable support. Since the term "reasonable" is apt to mean different things to different people, proposals for such support should be clarified as much as possible. Some plans charge for each service call. Others combine a series of types of support as in the third example. This is a highly negotiable issue and it is best to make sure that the clause in a particular license meets the needs of both licensor and licensee to the best possible degree. Since the amount of support needed

16. Support or Documentation (continued)

Clauses	Explanation	Cautions
b. Toll-free FAQ phone line with automated answers to common technical questions c. Regularly published newsletters, electronically accessed, with news and tips about the online almanacs d. Unlimited in-person no-charge technical support for the price of a toll call, available Monday through Friday 8am–6pm.		is difficult to determine, particularly when a licensee is leasing a new or unfamiliar product, some free-of-charge support should be negotiated.

17. Assignment

Clauses	Explanation	Cautions
This license Agreement shall not be assigned by any act of either licensor or licensee or by operation of the law. or *Neither party may assign this Agreement unless there is a written consent of the other party.*	This clause prevents the parties from assigning the license to another entity or provides a method for assignment. The clause is simple and clear.	There can be a proviso for assignment to a party's subsidiary or to an entity that purchases a party's assets. Such a proviso applies to the business providing the licensed product rather than the library, university, or school system. It should be noted that an assignment clause might forbid only the licensee from assigning the agreement. While it would be unusual for a library or school system to need equal ability to assign, it might happen (if a new school district were formed, for example). Therefore, an equal ability for both parties to assign, as in this example, makes for a better clause.

18. Waiver

Clauses	Explanation	Cautions
Failure on the part of either party to this Agreement to enforce a provision shall not constitute a waiver of that provision or of the right of the party to enforce that provision. Any waiver of a provision must be in writing (signed by the waiving party.) No breach is deemed consented to unless in writing (signed by the consenting party). Such consent does not constitute consent to any other breach.	This clause prevents the failure to enforce any provision of the license from being construed as a waiver of that or any other clause. This failure can be on the part of either the licensor or licensee. If a clause is to be waived, that must be indicated in writing and signed.	Simple failure to enforce a provision does not constitute a waiver. Ignoring a breach does not endorse the breach.

19. Severability

Clauses	Explanation	Cautions
Should any part of this Agreement be found to be illegal, unenforceable, or invalid, it shall be set aside and the rest of the Agreement shall remain in effect.	Easily read and understood, the severability clause protects the remainder of the Agreement if some part of the license is found to be problematic.	This contract clause is considered boiler plate—that is, it appears routinely in contracts. Nevertheless, it is important for the nonlawyer to know that the negation of one clause does not negate the rest of the document.

20. Confidentiality

Clauses	Explanation	Cautions
The licensee acknowledges and agrees that the terms and conditions of this Agreement shall be kept confidential at all times, and licensee shall not use or divulge such knowledge to any third party without the prior written consent of Zychon. The terms of this paragraph shall survive the expiration or early termination of this Agreement.	This clause concerns the licensor's attempt to keep some of the terms of the Agreement between parties from being revealed to others. The terms of the license are to be kept secret forever.	This kind of clause may hinder licensees who are interested in sharing information about the contracting process. Not an easy clause to live with, it is a deterrent to educating consumers in the electronic marketplace.

CLAUSES THAT APPEAR LESS FREQUENTLY

Examples of a number of other clauses that may or may not appear in a particular agreement are included here so that potential licensees can study the possibilities.

LESS-FREQUENT CLAUSES

1. Content and Copyright
2. Monitoring Use
3. Privacy Protection
4. Indemnification or Hold Harmless
5. Government Use
6. Amendments
7. *Force Majeure*
8. Signature Authority

---

1. Content and Copyright

Clauses	Explanation	Cautions
The licensee shall use reasonable care for the life of this Agreement in protecting Zychon's copyrights in the electronic almanac by allowing access only by authorized users for permitted uses.	This kind of clause has a number of variations. It is a way for the licensee to acknowledge that the licensor holds the rights to the copyrights involved with the leased materials. One variation of the clause includes a licensee duty to prevent excessive copying of the licensed product.	The "reasonable care" standard has no definition, so the licensee may have no guideline of what protections to put in place. However, the example offers some clarification through the requirement that limits its use to authorized users for permitted uses—and both terms are probably defined in other clauses or in the definitions section of the license agreement.

2. Monitoring Use

Although in some instances usage of a particular database or other electronic resource may be automatically measured, there are still many times when such automatic recording is not possible. Then the licensee may be asked to provide statistics on use to the licensor. If that happens, the kinds of user information collected and provided to the licensor must be such that the privacy of the users is protected. Consequently, licensee should never agree to furnish information about the material accessed by specific users. General statistics (such as the number of searches or downloads, and the types of site used—remote, dial-in, etc.) for a particular electronic product can be furnished. Information about which users are using what information should never be revealed— the best course is not to collect that kind of information even if it is obtainable.

How often a licensee must provide usage statistics to the licensor is something that should be carefully considered. Whether it is monthly, quarterly, or yearly can have a significant impact on the workload of the provider of the numbers. For some systems, frequent collection of statistical information may be easy, and possibly automatic. For others, it may be burdensome. Each situation is different and licensees should be cognizant of the ease or difficulty of statistics collection and transmittal. Licensee should not agree to a reporting system that is unduly burdensome.

Sharing usage numbers with the product provider can benefit the licensee; sometimes statistics prove helpful in negotiating lower prices or other benefits. On the other hand, these shared statistics could operate to the detriment of the licensee by providing the basis for increased pricing or reduction of other privileges.

In any case, it is clear that monitoring usage of a particular electron product is necessary for both the licensee and licensor, although the purposes for which such information is important may be different for each party.

2. Monitoring Use

Clauses	Cautions
Licensee shall provide Zychon with usage statistics each month for the previous month. These statistics shall be sent to the Zychon headquarters statistics department by the second Monday of the current month. Usage figures are to include total searches, the total time for all searches, the number of downloads, and the time(s) of day and day(s) of the month that are peak usage times. In addition, if there are users who are turned away because of busy signals, a description of those events are to be included in the statistical report.	There are other types of statistics that the licensor would find useful, such as the location of requests, the number of simultaneous users and so on. The possibilities are limitless, but caution is advised. Gathering such data can be time-consuming. However, both parties to a license may have great interest in these statistics.

3. Privacy Protection

Clauses	Explanation	Cautions
The privacy issues arises when the licensor puts a clause into the contract asking for information. It is the licensee's responsibility to review the request and decide—in the licensee's best guess—whether the information requested would be an invasion of the privacy of the users. If so, the licensee might agree to provide information in a different format. Because privacy is in the eye of the beholder, it is difficult to provide a sample privacy clause.	Some licenses include a clause wherein the licensor seeks detailed information about searchers and searches. There could even be a request for the name(s) of searchers, their status (e.g., student, staff member) and/or the specific information sought by the user.	If such a clause were included in a license, libraries and schools could be liable for invading the privacy of users. In fact, this kind of information should not be collected, even if it is not to be shared.
	The licensor might ask for the specific type of information requested, the purpose of the inquiry, and the type of user—student or faculty. If this information is supplied to the licensor, the licensee might be giving enough clues for the licensor to identify a patron. Instead, the licensee might agree to furnish the total number of searches during a time period without identifying the class of user, specific search queries, or any other user-identifying information.	Licensees should also avoid putting together "privacy clauses" stating that they will protect the privacy of their clientele. It is far better to simply not agree to furnish certain types of information proposed by the licensor. If licensees agree to protect the privacy of their clientele they are taking on an enormous burden and promising something over which they may not have control—for example the licensor may have ways of identifying users that the licensee does not know about.

4. Indemnification or Hold Harmless

Clauses	Explanation	Cautions
Licensee agrees to indemnify Zychon and to hold Zychon harmless from any and all claims of third parties that may arise relating to licensee's use of the licensed materials, regardless of whether or not such claims were foreseeable by the licensor.	Often the license has a clause in which the licensor states that there are no warranties on the quality and usability of the product being licensed (see limitation of liability clause). In addition to or instead of such a clause, another possible clause may appear, similar to the example here. It concerns indemnification—insulating the licensor—from all claims and burdening the licensee with responsibility should something go wrong. The user who is hurt in some way because the licensed material was wrong, or inaccurate, or out of date has no recourse with the licensor but must look to the license for relief.	This is an example of a clause that a licensee does not want. Don't expect the licensor to accept unlimited liability, but do expect some acceptance of liability. A clause that limits damages by type and amount can be acceptable. If the licensor is an aggregator (offering the products of more than one publisher), the clause may be written to protect both the aggregator and database providers (licensor and publishers).

5. Government Use

When the licensee is acting for a unit or agency of the United States government, special provisions apply. Because these provisions can change from time to time, those who are in such a situation should check carefully with their agency head to ensure compliance with the procedures and rules in effect for the licensing period.

6. Amendments

Clauses	Explanation	Cautions
Any amendment of or modification to this Agreement must be in writing and be agreed to and signed by the parties. or *The licensor may amend or modify the terms and/or conditions set forth in this Agreement upon written notice to the licensee.*	Many contracts, especially those that are for more than one year, have a clause that allows amendment of the document.	It is important that both parties to the license have the same right to propose modifications or amendments and that the agreement of the other party must be obtained. Some clauses do not have this parity for the parties. Such clauses as in the second example give the ability to change the terms or conditions set forth in the license to the licensor, but not to the licensee. This kind of one-sided privilege is obviously unacceptable.

7. Force Majeure

Clauses	Explanation	Cautions
With the exception of the payment of fees due, neither the licensor nor the licensee shall be liable for a failure or delay to perform if the failure or delay is the result of circumstances beyond the party's control and these circumstances are not due to the negligence or other misconduct of the party. Circumstances beyond the control of the parties may include national emergencies, fires, floods, Acts of God, an outbreak of war or insurrection, as well as the failure of carriers, subcontractors, or suppliers.	If some outside major force, such as the outbreak of war, or an Act of God, or even a failure brought about by a subcontractor, prevents the performance of contract obligations, this clause protects the nonperforming party from liability.	It is important that the clause be written to apply to both the licensee and the licensor.

8. Signature Authority

Clauses	Explanation	Cautions
The licensor and licensee warrant that the persons representing them in the signing of this Agreement are duly empowered to obligate them in this matter.	This clause seeks a guarantee that the person who signs for a party has the authority to do so. If a person signs the contract and lacks the proper authority to do so, a question about the validity of the contract may arise.	Libraries and schools should have evidence of an approved motion designating a signatory by the governing body, should it be needed. If the validity of the contract is questioned because of the signatory, it is possible that a finding by a court that the institution is not bound could lead to a personal suit against the signer. That is a truly scary scenario—one which is to be avoided at all cost. No one should sign a license of any kind for an institution unless he or she is authorized to do so and, therefore, is protected from being personally liable.

Part II
Making Decisions about
and
Negotiating Licensing
Agreements

4

Copyright or Licensing Agreement?

- *What three questions should be asked before accepting a licensing agreement?*
- *Under copyright law, can a software program be loaned by a library?*
- *Are libraries or archives ever permitted to copy a complete work?*

The growing use of shrink-wrap and webwrap licenses makes it almost impossible to use any electronic medium today without first accepting a licensing agreement. Often the only options available are either to accept the licensing agreement or not to access the material. Sometimes, however, there are other options.

The first question to ask before accepting a licensing agreement is whether this material is available elsewhere in an unlicensed form. For example, some material covered by the license may actually be in the public domain—no longer copyrighted. The material may also be available in another format that is not licensed, such as a book, government report, court case, or legislative proceeding. Also, permission might be secured to use copyrighted materials without licensing or paying of copyright fees—particularly if the use is for a limited time or purpose.

SCHOOL, LIBRARY, AND RESEARCHER RIGHTS UNDER COPYRIGHT LAW

The second question to ask, before accepting this licensing agreement, is what rights does the licensee have? In short, what rights do libraries, schools, and researchers have under copyright law? In general, these rights fall into five categories:

- the facts and ideas exception
- the first sale doctrine
- the doctrine of fair use
- the special rights granted to libraries and archives
- the Digital Millennium Copyright Act of 1998

The facts and ideas exception and the doctrine of fair use allow the use of portions of copyrighted materials, without first securing permission of the copyright owner or paying any licensing fee. The first sale doctrine allows the resale or loan of a copy of a copyrighted work after it is first sold, without payment of an additional fee to the copyright holder. The first sale doctrine is at the heart of such fundamental library activities as circulation of library materials. In fact, without the first sale doctrine, Friends of the Library groups could not hold fund-raising book sales without first securing licenses from book publishers or paying them fees. In addition to these rights, libraries and archives have their special rights granted to them exclusively by statute.

Facts and Ideas Exception[1]

Copyright statutes in the United States, up to and including the 1909 act, spoke about the exclusive rights of authors in absolute terms.[2] Despite the absolute language in the statutes, the courts developed doctrines on their own that limited copyright owners' exclusive rights. One of the earliest and most consistently held of these limitations has been the doctrine that facts and ideas cannot be copyrighted.[3] In 1991 the U.S. Supreme Court called this the "most fundamental axiom of copyright law."[4]

Even if a work is copyrighted, the facts and ideas that are a part of that work can still be used without the permission of the copyright owner. Only the author's particular expression of these facts and ideas is protected by copyright law. As the U.S. Supreme Court stated in 1991, "The mere fact that a work is copyrighted does not mean that every element of the work may be protected."[5]

The courts found the basis for this facts and ideas exception in the copyright clause of the U.S. Constitution:

> To promote the progress of science and useful arts by securing for a limited time to authors and inventors the exclusive right to their respective writings and discoveries.[6]

The courts have interpreted "authors" as those who are the originators, makers, or creators, and "writings" as that which they have originated.[7] "To qualify for copyright protection, therefore, a work must be original to the author."[8] It cannot be copied from another. Even when two works are almost identical, as long as each was independently created, both can be copyrighted.[9]

For a work to qualify as the writings of an author, therefore, the courts must determine that the work involved some kind of creative effort, no matter how modest that effort might be. Facts are not created; they are found.[10] Facts—including scientific, historical, biographical, and news facts—cannot therefore be copyrighted and must remain in the "public domain available to every person."[11] Facts existed before they were used in a copyrighted work and they would continue to exist even if they were not published in that work.[12]

However, while the underlying facts cannot be copyrighted, "the precise words used to present them"[13] cannot be copied without the copyright owner's permission. These words are original to their author. In 1985 the Supreme Court ruled that former President Ford could not prevent others from copying the bare historical facts in his autobiography but he could prevent others from copying his "subjective descriptions and portraits of public figures."[14]

The courts have also reasoned that granting a copyright to ideas would prevent others from using them and would thwart the copyright purpose statement of the Constitution, "To promote the progress of science and useful arts. . . . "

> The very object of publishing a book on science or the useful arts is to communicate to the world the useful knowledge it contains. But this object would be frustrated if the knowledge could not be used. . . . [15]

The idea limitation was incorporated in the 1976 act as section 102(b). In the House Report accompanying the bill it was made clear that this section "in no way enlarges or contracts the scope of copyright protection under the present law."[16]

First Sale Doctrine

The first sale doctrine had its origins in the English common law relating to the sale of real and personal property.[17] The doctrine was first affirmed by the U.S. courts in the 1894 case of *Harrison v. Maynard, Merrill & Co.*[18] In that case, unbound leaves of books had been damaged by fire in a bindery. The bindery then sold the damaged leaves as waste paper. However, a second-hand book dealer later acquired the leaves, had them bound, and then began selling them as books.

The Second Circuit Court of Appeals ruled that the copyright owner could not prevent the sale of the bound leaves. While it was true that the second-hand book dealer could not legally print or publish an edition of the books, once the bindery sold the damaged leaves, the dealer was free to resell those particular copies without compensation to the copyright owner.

The first sale doctrine was later affirmed by the U.S. Supreme Court in the 1908 case of *Bobbs-Merrill, Co. v. Straus D/B/A/* [doing business with] *R. H. Macy and Company.*[19]

Bobbs-Merrill, the publisher and copyright owner of a novel titled *The Castaway*, placed a notice in each copy just below the copyright notice, stating that:

> The price of this book at retail is one dollar net. No dealer is licensed to sell it at a less price, and a sale at less price will be treated as an infringement of the copyright.

To restrain R. H. Macy & Company from selling the novel at less than one dollar, Bobbs-Merrill Company brought suit. There was no contract or licensing agreement between the parties concerning the sale price. The court held that, while the copyright statute protects the copyright owners' right to copy and sell their works, the law does not create the right to limit the price at which their works are sold by future purchasers who are not bound by contract or agreement.[20]

The first sale doctrine was first codified as section 27 of the 1909 copyright law.[21] It appears today as section 109 of the copyright law.[22] Congress has placed limitations on phonorecords[23] and computer programs.[24] Phonorecords and computer programs cannot be rented, leased, or lent for direct or indirect commercial gain. Any person doing so is an infringer, subject to criminal penalties.

The only exceptions to these limitations on loaning phonorecords and computer programs are nonprofit libraries and educational institutions engaged in nonprofit lending. The current first sale doctrine holds that once such libraries or institutions have purchased (or have had purchased for them) any print medium (book, periodical, pamphlet, and so forth), phonorecord (LP record, audiotape, CD, DAT, or any new medium that may be invented), or piece of computer software (computer tape, disk, or other medium), they may lend that legally obtained copy without the permission of the copyright owner. For books and print matter, they may lend the original as many times as needed. In addition, they may make their own lending rules concerning the print material. There are some procedures that must be complied with concerning phonorecords and computer programs before they can

---

Figure 4.1. Warning of Copyright for Software Lending by Nonprofit Libraries

§201.24 Warning of copyright for software lending by nonprofit libraries.

(a) *Definition*. A Warning of Copyright for Software Rental is a notice under paragraph (b)(2)(A) of section 109 of the Copyright Act, title 17 of the United States Code, as amended by the Computer Software Rental Amendments Act of 1990, Public Law 101-650. As required by that paragraph, the "Warning of Copyright for Software Rental" shall be affixed to the package that contains the computer program which is lent by a nonprofit library for nonprofit purposes.

(b) *Contents*. A Warning of Copyright for Software Rental shall consist of a verbatim reproduction of the following notice, printed in such size and form and affixed in such manner as to comply with paragraph (c) of this section.

Notice: Warning of Copyright Restrictions

The copyright law of the United States (Title 17, United States Code) governs the reproduction, distribution, adaptation, public performance, and public display of copyrighted material.

Under certain circumstances specified in law, nonprofit libraries are authorized to lend, lease, or rent copies of computer programs to patrons on a nonprofit basis and for nonprofit purposes. Any person who makes an unauthorized copy or adaptation of the computer program, or redistributes the loan copy, or publicly performs or displays the computer program, except as permitted by title 17 of the United States Code, may be liable for copyright infringement.

This institution reserves the right to refuse to fulfill a loan request if, in its judgment, fulfillment of the request would lead to violation of the copyright law.

(c) *Form and manner of use*. A Warning of Copyright for Software Rental shall be affixed to the package that contains the copy of the computer program, which is the subject of a library loan to patrons, by means of a label cemented, gummed, or otherwise durably attached to the copies or to a box, reel, cartridge, cassette, or other container used as a permanent receptacle for the copy of the computer program. The notice shall be printed in such manner as to be clearly legible, comprehensible, and readily apparent to a casual user of the computer program.

[56 FR 7812, Feb. 26, 1991]

be lent, including affixing a copyright warning notice. The text of that warning notice appears in Figure 4.1.

Congress recently considered limiting the first sale doctrine for works of fine art and for exhibit photographs, but the final act[25] ended up only requiring a study of the problem.[26] The study was released in March 1996 and recommended that no further legislative action is necessary at this time. There have been no serious legislative attempts to repeal the first sale doctrine on books.

As a congressional committee stated, "The first sale doctrine represents an important balancing of interests."[27] A purchaser should be able to dispose of a lawfully owned copy without obtaining a copyright owner's permission or paying any additional fees. At the same time, the exclusive rights of copyright owners, except distribution, are still preserved. The first sale doctrine was limited in the commercial renting of phonorecords and software because of compelling evidence that it would seriously damage two very significant industries.[28] Congress, however, made it clear that passage of these particular narrow limitations on the first sale doctrine were to have no precedential value.[29] In fact, during the same congressional session in which commercial record rentals were prohibited, a proposal to limit home taping of copyrighted materials for private, noncommercial use was rejected.[30]

Fair Use

One of the most important legal limitations on authors' exclusive rights is the doctrine of fair use.[31] The need for this doctrine was first expressed by Lord Ellenborough in an 1803 case: "While I shall think myself bound to secure every man in the enjoyment of his copyright, one must not put manacles upon science."[32] This same thought was expressed by Judge Leval, who wrote in 1992 that the advancement of knowledge requires "some reasonable tolerance within which scholars and authors might freely use or quote from the writings of others for comment, criticism, debate, history, etc."[33]

The term "fair use" was actually first used in 1869,[34] but the doctrine received its classic formulation in 1841. Justice Story reasoned that to determine whether a use violates the copyright law, one must

> look to the nature and objects of the selections made, the quantity and value of the materials used and the degree in which the use may prejudice the sale or diminish the profits or supersede the objects of the original work.[35]

When the fair use doctrine was codified as section 107 of the 1976 copyright law,[36] Congress used Justice Story's formulation.[37]

The courts and Congress have found the rationale behind the fair use doctrine in the purpose statement of the copyright clause of the Constitution. The constitutional purpose in granting copyright protection in the first place[38] is "to promote the progress of science and the useful arts."[39] To serve that end, courts "must occasionally subordinate the copyright holder's interest in a maximum financial return to the greater public interest in the development of art, science and industry."[40] In addition, as Justice Story explained,

> in truth, in literature, in science and in art, there are, and can be, few, if any, things, which in an abstract sense, are strictly new and original throughout. Every book in literature, science and art, borrows, and must necessarily borrow, and use much which was well known and used before.[41]

Fair use allows copying of copyrighted works without the owner's permission for purposes such as "criticism, comment, news reporting, teaching (including multiple copies for classroom use), scholarship, or research. . . . "[42] Four factors are used to determine if a use is fair:

- the purpose and the character of the use, including whether such use is of a commercial nature or is for nonprofit educational purposes

- the nature of the copyrighted work
- the amount and substantiality of the portion used in relation to the copyrighted work as a whole
- the effect of the use upon the potential market for or value of the copyrighted work

To help educators, "Guidelines for Educational Fair Use"[43] were agreed upon by representatives from the Ad Hoc Committee of Educational Institutions and Organizations on Copyright Revision; the Authors League of America; and the Association of American Publishers. These guidelines are for classroom copying in nonprofit educational institutions and apply to the copying of both books and periodicals.

Special Rights Granted to Libraries and Archives

Section 108 of the copyright law extends special privileges to qualifying libraries and archives. Entitled "Limitations on Exclusive Rights: Reproduction by Libraries and Archives," it allows libraries and archives that meet certain criteria to make and/or distribute copies of printed materials. Not only does this section make it possible for libraries to copy whole works for certain reasons, but it also allows copying for interlibrary loan to fill patron requests. And, of course, it is important to remember that section 108 privileges coexist with section 107, the fair use doctrine. One right does not preclude or cancel the other.

Digital Millennium Copyright Act of 1998[44]

To update the copyright law to deal with new technologies, and in order for the United States to join two World Intellectual Property Organization treaties concluded in Geneva in December of 1996, Congress enacted the Digital Millennium Copyright Act of 1998. Among its provisions are an exemption that allows nonprofit libraries, archives, or educational institutions to circumvent copyright protection systems to access material for the purpose of determining if it wishes to acquire a copy.[45] A copy of the provisions relating to libraries and archives appears in Appendix B.

MAKING THE DECISION

The third and final question to be answered before accepting a licensing agreement is: which is better—your rights under copyright or under the licensing agreement? This question can only be answered by a careful reading of the licensing agreement. While some licensing agreements state that "nothing in this agreement affects rights under the copyright law," the majority are silent on the issue. It must be determined from the effects of the terms of the agreement whether fair use and other rights are still relevant.

Most significantly, the Digital Millennium Copyright Act of 1998 contains provisions preserving fair use after a user has gained authorized access to a work. Section 1201 (see Appendix B) distinguishes between access-prevention technology and infringement-prevention technology, and

> does not contain a prohibition against individual acts of circumvention of the latter. As a result, an individual would not be able to circumvent in order to gain unauthorized access to a work, but would be able to do so in order to make fair use of a work which she has lawfully acquired. Second, it contains a savings clause that explicitly preserves fair use and other exceptions to rights in the Copyright Act.[46]

Nevertheless, it is yet to be determined how copyright owners will react to the new law.[47] No one should ever give up his or her rights under copyright law in any licensing agreement just for expedience. These rights are just too important.

NOTES

1. The Collection of Information Anti-Privacy Act did not pass in the 105th Congress. This bill would have provided protection to facts in databases.

2. The 1790 Act [Chapter XV, 1 Stat. 124 (May 31, 1790)] declared that copyright owners had the "*sole* right and liberty of printing, reprinting, publishing and vending such map, chart, book or books. . . . " [emphasis added]. The 1870 Act [16 Stat. 198 §86 (July 8, 1870)] added "completing, copying, executing, finishing" to the list. The 1909 Act, which remained in effect through 1977, further increased the list of "exclusive rights" and added only one limitation—the first sale doctrine. It was not until the 1976 Act [90 Stat. 2541 (October 19, 1976)] that an enumeration of "various limitations, qualifications, or exemptions" (H.R. No. 94-1476, 61–62) actually became part of the copyright statute.

3. *Baker v. Selden*, 101 U.S. 99 (1897).

4. *Feist Publication, Inc. v. Rural Telephone Service*, 499 U.S. 340 (1991), at 344.

5. *Feist*, 348.

6. U.S. Const., Art. 1, §8, cl. 8.

7. *Burrow-Giles Lithographic Co. v. Savony*, 111 U.S. 53, at 58 (1884), observed that:

   By writings in that clause is meant the literary productions of those authors, and Congress very properly has declared these to include all forms of writing, printing, engraving, etching, &c., by which the ideas in the mind of the author are given visible expression.

8. *Feist*, 345.

9. Ibid., 346.

10. "The first person to find and report a particular fact has not created the fact; he or she has merely discovered its existence." Ibid., 347.

11. *Miller v. Universal City Studios, Inc.*, 650 F.2d 1365 at 1369 (1981).

12. *Feist*, 361.

13. Ibid., 348.

14. *Harper & Row, Publishers, Inc. v. National Enterprises*, 471 U.S. 539, at 556–557.

15. *Baker*, 103.

16. House Report No. 94-1476 (Committee on the Judiciary) 14.

17. "The first sale doctrine has its roots in the English common law rule against restraints on alienation of property." House Report No. 98-987 (to accompany H.R. 5938), 2.

18. 51 F. 689.

19. 210 U.S. 339.

20. Ibid., at 350.

21. 17 U.S.C. §27 (1909) states:

    The copyright is distinct from the property in the material object copyrighted, and the sale or conveyance, by gift or otherwise, of the material object shall not of itself constitute a transfer of the title to the material object: but nothing in this title shall be deemed to forbid, prevent, or restrict the transfer of any copy of a copyrighted work the possession of which has been lawfully obtained.

22. Titled *Limitations on exclusive rights: Effect of transfer of particular copy or phonorecord*, the section reads simply:

(a) Notwithstanding the provisions of section 106(3), the owner of a particular copy or phonorecord lawfully made under this title, or any person authorized by such owner, is entitled, without the authority of the copyright owner, to sell or otherwise dispose of the possession of that copy or phonorecord.

23. Record Rental Act of 1984, P.L. 98-450.
24. Computer Software Rental Amendments Act of 1990, P.L. 101-650.
25. Visual Artists Rights Act of 1990, P.L. 101-650.
26. The report was done by Marybeth Peters, Register of Copyrights, and is titled, *Waiver of Moral Rights in Visual Artworks—Final Report of the Register of Copyrights* (Library of Congress, U.S. Copyright Office). It is available from the Government Printing Office.
27. House Report (Judiciary Committee) No. 101-735, September 21, 1990 (to accompany H.R. 101-735 (September 1990), 7.
28. House Report (Judiciary Committee) No. 98-987, August 31, 1984 (to accompany H.R. 5938), 2.
29. Ibid.
30. Ibid.
31. Notes of the Committee on the Judiciary, House Report No. 94-1476. "The judicial doctrine of fair use, one of the most important and well-established limitations on the exclusive right of copyright owners, would be given express statutory recognition for the first time in section 107."
32. *Carey v. Kearsley*, 4 Esp. 168, at 170.
33. *American Geophysical Union v. Texaco, Inc.*, 802 F. Supp. 1, at 10.
34. *Lawrence v. Dana*, 15 F. Cas. 26 (C.C.D. Mass.).
35. 9 F. Cas. 342, at 348.
36. As stated in *Sony Corp. of America v. Universal Studios, Inc.*, 464 U.S. 417, at 447 n. 29:

The Copyright Act of 1909, 35 Stat. 1075, did not have a "fair use" provision. Although that Act's compendium of exclusive rights "to print, reprint, publish, copy, and vend the copyrighted work" was broad enough to encompass virtually all potential interactions with a copyrighted work, the statute was never so construed. The courts simply refused to read the statute literally in every situation. When Congress amended the statute in 1976, it indicated that it "intended to restate the present judicial doctrine of fair use, not to change, narrow, or enlarge it in any way." H.R. No. 94-1476, 66 (1976).

37. The first factor, the purpose and character of the use, was drawn from "the objects of the selections made ... and the degree in which the use ... may supersede the objects of the original work." The second factor, the nature of the copyrighted work, from "nature ... of the selections made ... and the degree in which the use may ... supersede the objects of the original work." The third factor, the amount and substantiality of the portion used, was drawn from "the quantity ... of the materials used and the degree in which the use may ... supersede the objects of the original work." The fourth factor, the effect of the

use on the potential market for the copyright, from "degree in which the use may prejudice the sale or diminish the profits. . . . "

38. *Mathews Conveyor Co. v. Palmer-Bee Co.*, 135 F.2d 73 (1943).
39. U.S. Constitution, Art I, §8, cl. 8.
40. *Berlin v. E. C. Publications, Inc.*, 329 F.2d 541, at 544 (1964).
41. *Emerson v. Davies*, 8 F. Cas. 615, 619 (No. 4,436) (CCD Mass. 1845).
42. 17 U.S.C. §107.
43. House Report No. 94–1476 (1976).
44. P.L. 105-304, signed by President Clinton on October 28, 1998.
45. 17 U.S.C. § 1201(d) Exemption for Nonprofit Libraries, Archives, and Educational Institutions.
46. See Testimony of Mary Beth Peter, Register of Copyright, before the House Subcommittee on Courts and Intellectual Property in support of H.R. 2180 and H.R. 2281, September 16, 1997.
47. Ibid.

Other critical questions are whether, as a practical matter, copyright owners will adopt reasonable terms for granting lawful access, including recognition of fair use interests; whether copyrighted works will remain available in formats other than electronic, encrypted form to be used for fair use purposes; and whether any technological means will be developed to allow individuals to circumvent for lawful purposes.

5
Negotiating the License

- *Under what circumstances are shrink-wrap licenses negotiable?*
- *What is the best advice for negotiating a licensing agreement?*
- *Why is it important to watch out for the "no library loan" clause in an agreement negotiated for a consortium? What if it's there?*

ARE ALL LICENSES NEGOTIABLE?

In earlier chapters, we looked at the different types of licenses and some common clauses. Shrink-wrap and webwrap licenses were described as take-it-or-leave-it licenses. Licenses that are negotiated clause by clause seem, at first glance, to be the only ones that can be negotiated.

Under specific circumstances, however, both shrink-wrap and webwrap licenses may be negotiable. The shrink-wrap license enclosed in the software package and purchased by an individual at the computer store in the mall is set in its terms and conditions. There is no reasonable way whereby the software producer could negotiate an individualized license with each and every one of the thousands of customers who purchase that software in a given year.

However, that same shrink-wrap license may not be appropriate or acceptable for a library, research organization, university, or school system. Software producers know this and are usually amenable to a negotiated license for a software package that typically comes with a shrink-wrap license—if it is to be used by a number of individuals or at a number of sites instead by one individual at one site. It's important to know this, because it means that even those licenses that seem to be nonnegotiable may be, at least in part, negotiable.

Webwrap licenses may be negotiable as well. Again, the circumstances surrounding the use to be made of the licensed resource may allow for the possibility of changing, dropping, or adding clauses.

Thus, the shrink-wrap license or the webwrap license may fall into the negotiable-clause-by-clause category under certain circumstances.

THE NEGOTIATION PROCESS

The negotiation process begins with a communication of some kind. The potential licensee may, for example, contact the potential licensor to indicate an interest in obtaining the licensed resource. Or the representative of the company that has a product to offer may visit or otherwise contact the potential customer. E-mails may be exchanged. Whatever form communication takes, it is the first step in what could turn into a negotiated agreement.

It is usual in the business of licensing electronic resources that the license is a document offered by the licensor. The licensee then reacts to the document. This approach may change over time, as model licenses are generated cooperatively between the producers of electronic tools and their users. Librarians, in particular, are concerned about this area in which expertise is needed, and they are cooperating as much as possible to help each other arrive at fair terms. There is some talk of making model licenses available through the Internet, and there are now some sites where potential licensees can look at possible contract clauses. Often interpretations of the clauses are included. Tips on what is and is not acceptable in a clause are also available. The Yale site (www.library.yale.edu/~llicense/intro.shtml), the University of Texas site (www.utsystem.edu/ogc/intellectualproperty/contract/techc.htm), and the ARL site (http:arl.cni.org/scomm/licensing/licbooklet.html) are good resources for librarians. Large universities, such as the University of California, may have information on licensing available on their Web sites. Other sites may be found by using one of the Web search engines or crawlers to search for "licensing agreements" or some variation of that phrase.

The producers of electronic products need customers, but they also need to protect their proprietary rights. Librarians, researchers, and educators need these electronic products to carry on their work, but they also need to protect the rights that adhere under the copyright law and that enable them to carry on their work effectively. The more producers and users can understand each other's rights, responsibilities, and needs, the more likely it is that licenses will become easier to read and understand, as well as more equitable.

Because there are no standard licenses, although there are similarities among the various licenses, care is needed from the start. The product producer generally has a license ready to offer to the potential user. This license is developed by the producer's attorney and it protects the interests of the licensor. It is the potential licensee's responsibility to consider carefully the licensing terms and conditions to determine their acceptability.

Ideally, the licensee would have access to an attorney experienced in licensing. Since that is not usually the case, the licensee must become educated in the terms and conditions of such agreements. Tools that aid in such a task are legal dictionaries, books of standard legal forms, and Internet sites such as those listed above. Talking, meeting, or e-mailing with other licensees is one of the best ways to learn about the ins and outs of licensing. Such networking may take place at meetings, conferences, or workshops, or in other venues such as listservs. If a license does not include a glossary, it might be helpful to ask that one be added to the license. In addition, asking the licensor to explain what a clause, word, or phrase means is an appropriate route to take. Queries of this sort can lead to "plain-language" clauses.

WILL A LICENSOR ALWAYS NEGOTIATE TERMS AND CONDITIONS?

A licensor may decide not to negotiate any of the terms and conditions set forth in the licensing document generated by his or her attorney. That is certainly the privilege of the licensor who holds the rights to the electronic resource. If, for example, the licensor is the sole provider for a product and there is nothing similar on the market, that is a powerful position to be in. Or, there may be some other reason for the product owner to refuse to change anything in the license. In either case, the potential licensee has to weigh the pros and cons of acceding to the terms or going without the product.

Generally, however, the market dictates that a reasonable approach for the licensor is to listen to the customer and to make accommodations where feasible. Negotiation may not always work, but it does most of the time.

HOW TO NEGOTIATE AS A POTENTIAL LICENSEE

"Read the document" is the best advice for any potential licensee. "Read the document and get clarification for those areas that you don't understand" is even better advice. Understanding what the clauses say is the key to obtaining a license that works. Before negotiating any license for a resource, it is also essential to know the intended users and uses, any budgetary constraints, the viability of maintaining or dispensing with similar or like resources, what resources and levels of access are needed, and a host of other factors.

All publicly funded agencies and institutions need policies and processes for timely license review and approval. Large libraries and educational institutions will have a legal firm on retainer or a legal officer who will be part of the review process. Smaller libraries, colleges, or school systems may not have access to such an advisor, but it is important for any of these organizations to think carefully before proceeding to negotiate a license without expert help.

The process of clause-by-clause license negotiation begins with the receipt (in the mail, by fax, or electronically) of the proposed license. Armed with the knowledge of what the licensor expects, the potential licensee can begin review.

A careful review process is recommended—preferably it consists of a reading of the license clauses by a number of people selected by the licensee. Each reader makes notes, indicating questions, omissions, unacceptable wording or clauses, lack of clarity, difficult language, ambiguities, unnecessary clauses, and so forth.

A meeting of those who have read the contract is then held, allowing each reader to bring his or her concerns to the table. Someone at the meeting is responsible for taking notes, and all of the readers' concerns are later brought to the appropriate parties for clarification. Sometimes clarification comes from the licensor; sometimes departments not involved in the actual negotiations furnish answers to questions; and sometimes legal counsel is needed.

While such a review process is time-consuming, especially for the first licenses, as staff gains experience, the process becomes quicker and easier. Until recently, many of those who faced a potential license found it overwhelming. The language seemed impenetrable ("Since when are my students 'third-party users?' "), the terminology mystifying ("What on earth is merchantability and fitness?"), and the responsibilities awesome ("How can I hold the licensor harmless for what is clearly his or her fault?"). But as licensees gain experience in reading licenses, the language becomes less of a mystery and the clauses become familiar. Patterns emerge. People know what to look for. Print sources such as legal dictionaries become routine tools of the trade. URLs that may contain helpful information are bookmarked for easy reference. The review process takes less time.

Once the review process is complete, the person responsible for dealing with the vendor (or producer, or licensor) conveys the agency's concerns about the license. If there are proposed changes to license clauses, these are sent, in writing, to the licensor. Alternatively, a meeting is held where both parties to the contract look at the requested changes.

It is important, when negotiations are ready to begin, that the licensee's institutional representative be given clear guidance as to what clauses or wording are unacceptable. Backstop positions should be in place since the licensee may not be able to obtain every concession being sought. However, the most important changes should be identified and be the object of the most determined bargaining.

Once the bargaining process is concluded, the final version of the license is drawn up and reviewed by all concerned. Then the signatures of the authorized representatives for both parties are affixed and both parties live with the document for the specified length of time.

The process described above is for a negotiated-clause-by-clause license. If an organization is considering a product that comes with a shrink-wrap license, it is wise to contact the product producer or the vendor and request a copy of the license. That license may be perfectly acceptable. However, if some clauses violate the organization's procedure or policy, the situation might be remedied by contacting the licensor, sometimes through a vendor. Nothing ventured, nothing gained. If the licensor indicates a willingness to consider revising any of the shrink-wrap license clauses, the process described for clause-by-clause license negotiation is appropriate.

The same approach can also be used with a webwrap license. The potential licensee should go to the producer's Web page, study the license clauses, and determine whether they are acceptable. If they are not, the licensee should contact the licensor to see what, if anything, can be done.

BANDING TOGETHER—A BETTER WAY TO GO?

While the in-house review process, described above, can work for some organizations, going it alone is not always the best way to negotiate licensing agreements.

One way to develop negotiating clout is for institutions to band together. Some consortia are established solely for the purpose of negotiating licenses. There is *always* power in numbers—especially in budget numbers. Sometimes, the group hires someone specifically to negotiate the best deal for the membership.

It is wise, however, to proceed with caution when negotiating a license for a group. Some consortia are getting better pricing schemes by agreeing to a "no library loan" clause or by agreeing to give up their fair use rights. While lower prices may make the members of the consortium happy, agreeing to a "no library loan" clause clearly raises the issue of "have" and "have-not." If, for example, the libraries that "have" are willing to forego interlibrary loan privileges to save money, the libraries that "have not" may have nowhere to turn when their patrons need information. Such an arrangement is clearly contrary to the basic mission of libraries; what appears to be a simple cost-saving strategy thus has serious ramifications for the very survival of library services in the new millennium.

Appendix A:
Checklist for Evaluating Licenses

Here is a checklist that can be helpful in determining the feasibility of clauses or portions of clauses in a proposed license. The checklist may also help in developing alternative clauses or phrases to replace or add to those in a proposed license. Finally, it serves as a reminder of the possible areas that need to be covered.

____Are the parties correctly identified?

____Is the licensor a sole source for this type of product?

____Are terms defined? Are the definitions commonly used and easily understood?

____Are authorized users identified appropriately?

____Are the permitted uses clearly defined and satisfactory?

____Is access via all sites, including remote sites, included in the license?

____Are the licensed materials identified fully?

____Are fair use and other copyright privileges intact?

____Are payment and fee schedules spelled out?

____Are the electronic products tied to the purchase of a print version of the product?

____Is the pricing for the product competitive?

____Are costs easily determined?

____Are there staff training costs associated with use of this product?

____Are there user training costs associated with use of this product?

____Are there new or additional hardware, software, and/or telecommunications costs?

____Is there quality control?

____Is the license term (length) defined and acceptable?

____Is there automatic renewal?

____Is renewal based on agreement of the parties?

____Is there provision for fee schedule adjustment (downward as well as upward) upon renewal?

____Is there need for increased staffing?

____Is there possibility of decreased staffing?

____Is there need for new categories of staffing?

_____ Is technical support available at the necessary times?

_____ Is the technical support free?

_____ Are there various levels of technical support?

_____ Are there prohibitions on

    _____ disassembling?

    _____ reverse engineering?

    _____ decompiling?

    _____ reproducing?

    _____ leasing?

    _____ distributing?

_____ Does the licensor disclaim liability for

    _____ quality?

    _____ performance?

    _____ merchantability?

    _____ fitness for a particular purpose?

    _____ suitability?

    _____ correctness?

    _____ accuracy?

____reliability?

____Does licensee bear entire risk regarding

____quality?

____performance?

____suitability?

____correctness?

____accuracy?

____reliability?

____Are there interlibrary loan privileges?

____Is there a termination clause according either party the same rights?

____Is the governing law for dispute resolution that of the licensee's state, the licensor's state, or some other state?

____Is alternative dispute resolution available or mandated?

____Is there cost sharing for alternative dispute resolution?

____Is assignment only in writing?

____Are there waiver and severability clauses?

____Can the license be amended?

____If it can be amended, is the process acceptable?

____Is there an indemnification or hold harmless clause?

____Is there a demand for usage statistics?

____Do the usage statistics requirements invade the users' privacy?

____Is there a requirement to monitor use?

____Does the licensor restrict sharing information about the terms and conditions of the license?

____Is there a requirement for the licensee to protect copyright and other proprietary rights of the licensor?

____If so, is it reasonable to guarantee to protect those rights?

____Are there online links to third-party sites?

____If so, is the licensor responsible for the quality of those linked sites?

____Is the licensor responsible for the content of those linked sites?

____Is there a natural disaster and wars (force majeure) clause?

____Is the signatory for the licensor authorized?

____Is the signatory for the licensee authorized?

____Is the agreement complete and entire and in writing?

Appendix B:
Digital Millennium
Copyright Act of 1998
Provisions Relating to Libraries and Archives

TITLE I—WIPO TREATIES IMPLEMENTATION

Sec. 103. Copyright Protection Systems and Copyright Management Information

CHAPTER 12—COPYRIGHT PROTECTION AND MANAGEMENT SYSTEMS

Sec. 1201. Circumvention of copyright protection systems

* * *

(c) OTHER RIGHTS, ETC., NOT AFFECTED- (1) Nothing in this section shall affect rights, remedies, limitations, or defenses to copyright infringement, including fair use, under this title.

(d) EXEMPTION FOR NONPROFIT LIBRARIES, AR-CHIVES, AND EDUCATIONAL INSTITUTIONS- (1) A nonprofit library, archives, or educational institution which gains access to a commercially exploited copyrighted work solely in order to make a good faith determination of whether to acquire a copy of that work for the sole purpose of engaging in conduct permitted under this title shall not be in violation of subsection (a)(1)(A). A copy of a work to which access has been gained under this paragraph—

(A) may not be retained longer than necessary to make such good faith determination; and

(B) may not be used for any other purpose.

(2) The exemption made available under paragraph (1) shall only apply with respect to a work when an identical copy of that work is not reasonably available in another form.

(3) A nonprofit library, archives, or educational institution that willfully for the purpose of commercial advantage or financial gain violates paragraph (1)—

(A) shall, for the first offense, be subject to the civil remedies under section 1203; and

(B) shall, for repeated or subsequent offenses, in addition to the civil remedies under section 1203, forfeit the exemption provided under paragraph (1).

(4) This subsection may not be used as a defense to a claim under subsection (a)(2) or (b), nor may this subsection permit a nonprofit library, archives, or educational institution to manufacture, import, offer to the public, provide, or otherwise traffic in any technology, product, service, component, or part thereof, which circumvents a technological measure.

(5) In order for a library or archives to qualify for the exemption under this subsection, the collections of that library or archives shall be—

(A) open to the public; or

(B) available not only to researchers affiliated with the library or archives or with the institution of which it is a part, but also to other persons doing research in a specialized field.

* * *

Sec. 1203. Civil remedies

* * *

(c) AWARD OF DAMAGES-

* * *

(5) Innocent violations-
NONPROFIT LIBRARY, ARCHIVES, OR EDUCA-
TIONAL INSTITUTIONS- In the case of a nonprofit library, archives, or educational institution, the court shall
remit damages in any case in which the library, archives,
or educational institution sustains the burden of prov-
ing, and the court finds, that the library, archives, or
educational institution was not aware and had no reason to believe that its acts constituted a violation.

Sec. 1204. Criminal offenses and penalties

* * *

(b) LIMITATION FOR NONPROFIT LIBRARY, AR-
CHIVES, OR EDUCATIONAL INSTITUTION—Subsec-
tion (a) shall not apply to a nonprofit library, archives,
or educational institution.

* * *

TITLE IV—MISCELLANEOUS PROVISIONS

* * *

Sec. 404. Exemption for Libraries and Archives.—
Section 108 of title 17, United States Code, is amended—
(2) in subsection (b)—
(A) by striking 'a copy or phonorecord' and inserting 'three copies or phonorecords';
(B) by striking 'in facsimile form'; and
(C) by striking 'if the copy or phonorecord reproduced is currently in the collections of the library or archives.' and inserting 'if—
   (1)   the copy or phonorecord reproduced is currently in the collections of the library or archives'; and
   (2)   'any such copy or phonorecord that is reproduced in digital format is not otherwise distributed in that format and is not made available to the public in that format outside the premises of the library or archives'; and
   (3)   in subsection (c)—
      (A)   by striking 'a copy or phonorecord' and inserting 'three copies or phonorecords';
      (B)   by striking 'in facsimile form';
      (C)   by inserting 'or if the existing format in which the work is stored has become obsolete,' after 'stolen,';
      (D)   by striking 'if the library or archives has, after a reasonable effort, determined that an unused replacement cannot be obtained at a fair price.' and inserting 'if—
         (1)   the library or archives has, after a reasonable effort, determined that an unused replacement cannot be obtained at a fair price; and
         (2)   any such copy or phonorecord that reproduced in digital format is not made available to the public in that format

outside the premises of the library or archives in lawful possession of such copy'; and

(E) by adding at the end the following: 'For purposes of this subsection, a format shall be considered obsolete if the machine or device necessary to render perceptible a work stored in that format is no longer manufactured or is no longer reasonably available in the commercial marketplace.'

Appendix C:
International Coalition of Library Consortia (ICOLC) *Statement of Current Perspective and Preferred Practices for the Selection and Purchase of Electronic Information*

Publishers today increasingly act globally to provide electronic information, and it is incumbent upon libraries to act globally to express their market positions on the pricing and other terms and conditions related to the purchase of that information. This document sets forth concerns about the current electronic information environment, the desired environment for the future, and the preferred practices for library consortia and their member libraries to achieve the desired outcomes. In a rapidly changing technology and information environment, the general goals and views outlined here will remain relatively constant, while the specific terms may change based upon experience.

Although this statement may have general applicability, the adopters expect that its primary relevance will be within the higher education community. A premise of this document is that the current scholarly communication system will continue during the critical transition period from print publication to electronic distribution of scholarly and research materials. Our primary intention is to define the current conditions and preferred practices for pricing and delivering scholarly information within this emerging electronic environment. While other organizations have set forth useful proposals that offer the potential to change significantly the structure of the scholarly certification and review process [1], those efforts go beyond our current scope. This statement builds upon and complements the work of others to develop principles for the licensing of electronic resources. [2]

This statement aims to provide a starting point for a dialog among information providers and library consortia. The members of ICOLC invite information providers to engage in meaningful discussions about how this document might help advance ubiquitous and affordable information resources for library users in educational and research institutions.

Definition of Terms. The following terms, which may have both general and specific definitions in other contexts, are used within this document as follows:

E-information (or electronic information). A broad term that encompasses abstracting and indexing services, electronic journals and other full text materials, the offerings of information aggregators, article delivery services, etc. E-information can be accessed via remote networks from information providers, or locally mounted by a consortium or one of its member libraries.

Fair Use. Used here not to describe the specific copyright laws or guidelines of any one country, but rather the general principle of a society's lawfully permitted copying or excerpting of copyrighted materials in the course of education, scholarship, commentary, or to advance learning and other societal goals. Fair use can be made without the user's paying a specific fee or needing to seek the copyright owner's permission. (Used interchangeably with the term "fair dealing" that is more commonly used in Canada, Australia and the United Kingdom.)

Providers (or information providers). Includes traditional print and electronic scholarly publishers (both for-profit and not-for-profit), trade publishers, information aggregators and other vendors, and other electronic-only information disseminators.

I.   INTRODUCTION.

A.   The goal of academic libraries is to meet the teaching, learning, scholarly, research, and other information needs of their faculty, students, and affiliates, and to do so effectively and efficiently.

B.   E-information resources are very much in a developmental phase. Therefore, this statement is a work in progress rather than a final product.

C.   While this statement intends to be broad enough to encompass all types of academic consortia, and to set general boundaries within which consortia usually operate, experimentation is necessary and encouraged within this emerging field. Therefore, this statement is not intended to preclude individual consortia from taking specific actions that may be appropriate to their own needs.

II.   CURRENT PROBLEMS AND NEEDS FOR THE FUTURE.

This section addresses a number of key issues that have an impact upon the provision of electronic information (and electronic journals in particular):

A. Increasing Expectations and Stable Budgets.

Current Problem: Over time, academic institutions typically have spent a decreasing percentage of their educational and general budgets on their libraries. Nonetheless, academic institutions and library clients expect their libraries to obtain new electronic resources while simultaneously maintaining or growing traditional print collections until the electronic resources are fully stable. Libraries also are expected to do this with no additional funding.

Future Need: Academic libraries and information providers must use information technologies to facilitate increased information delivery and to make e-information more generally, readily, and flexibly accessible than its print counterpart.

B. Fair Use Under Attack.

Current Problem: Although there exists no empirical evidence that fair use causes material or undue harm to providers, many information providers nonetheless are seeking to discontinue the well-established principle of fair use, and they are using the new electronic environment as the reason and means to do so.

Future Need: The concept of fair use continues to be relevant and must be retained in the electronic environment.

C. Archiving of Information.

Current Problem: Print publications provide a degree of permanence that is critical to academic libraries. However, if not managed properly, e-information can be highly transient.

Future Need: It is critical to libraries and the constituents they serve that permanent archival access to information be available, especially if that information exists only in electronic form. Libraries cannot rely solely on external providers to be their archival source. Therefore, agreements to procure e-information must include provisions to purchase and not just to lease or provide temporary access.

D. Changes to the Scholarly Communications System to Meet the Needs of Teaching, Learning, and Research.

Current Problem: Academic libraries are but one of several key players in a large, complex scholarly communications system that is becoming dysfunctional. Symptoms of such dysfunction include: an increasing volume of academic journal publication (particularly in science, technology and medicine) that is redundant or repetitive, and that is generated as much for the certification (through tenure and promotion) of authors as for the advancement of learning; the inability of academic institutional budgets to support the growing number of research journal publications; the push by some publishers to increase profit by charging high prices for catering to the academic research trade; the clash of values in the copyright ownership of academic works; and the reluctance by many sectors, including academic authors, to deploy the new technologies to improve the current scholarly communications system.

Future Need: Scholars, academic institutions, publishers, and libraries should share a common and compelling interest in fostering systems of publishing that result in broad information access at an affordable price. To achieve this, each group must take steps to improve the current system. *Universities and colleges* must modify recognition and rewards systems to create disincentives for unnecessary publication. *Publishers* must charge reasonable prices for journal subscriptions. *Academic libraries* must purchase subscriptions only to journal titles of certain value to scholarship and learning. *Academic authors* must develop an understanding of how copyright law works and how to use their ownership, the law, and fair use provisions to support the work of scholarly creation and dissemination. *All parties* must be willing to take risks to create and implement new, technologically enabled research outlets for initial publication of scholarship and research results.

E.   Pricing Strategies.

Current Problem: Current pricing models for e-information, which are developing during a period of experimentation, are not sustainable. While present pricing approaches of information providers may in some cases be desirable as a bridging strategy to the future, academic libraries, with their diminishing fiscal resources, will rapidly be unable to afford to support the pricing strategies for electronic information currently advocated by information providers. For example, academic libraries cannot afford to commit long-term to the now-prevalent electronic journal pricing model that is premised upon a base price of "current print price *plus* electronic surcharge *plus* significant projected inflation surcharges." Furthermore, today's electronic information products are neither fully formed nor stable, yet libraries are being asked to support in full the cost of the research and development to bring such products to market.

Future Need: Pricing models for e-information must result in a significant reduction in the per use (or "unit cost") of information. The savings accrued through the production of electronic information should, over time, be passed from the provider to the customer. Eventually, the methods for pricing electronic information must dovetail with the financial requirements of information providers and the budgets and missions of academic libraries. Additionally, academic library consortia must work with information providers to reduce the overall cost of electronic information so the member libraries can demonstrate that they are delivering more services at the same cost. Strategies for doing so may include increasing the total number of uses of the electronic information above that for the print publication, or reducing the base cost to obtain the information.

F.   Measures of Effectiveness.

Current Problem: Neither academic libraries nor information providers have sufficient experience or data to determine the appropriate unit cost of information, the effective return on investment, or the most appropriate economic model for charging or paying for electronic information. Academic libraries cannot afford to purchase information that is not of proven need on campus.

Future Need: Effective data must be collected and measures of success must be constantly reevaluated. Libraries and providers must jointly develop and agree upon what constitutes an effective measure of the use and value of electronic information so both parties can demonstrate better returns on investment. Improved measures of e-information effectiveness will be essential to enable libraries to secure future funding to procure these resources.

III. PREFERRED PRACTICES IN THE EMERGING ELECTRONIC INFORMATION ENVIRONMENT.

A. Contract Negotiations.

1. Providers should not preclude libraries from working through consortia to seek advantageous pricing or other special arrangements by writing contracts only with individual institutions and not with consortia.

2. All terms and conditions should be negotiated and clearly stated in the contract. Hidden charges, after-the-fact retroactive charges, changes in content, or any other changes in commitment are not acceptable without renegotiation.

3. Non-disclosure language, if necessary, should not preclude library consortia from sharing pricing and other significant terms and conditions with other consortia.

B. Pricing.

1. Recognizing that libraries have limited new funds to invest in e-information (including electronic journals), and that providers are not yet providing fully debugged and client-ready electronic products (especially electronic journals), providers should not engage in excessive pricing during the current period of experimentation. Therefore:

a. Consortia and their libraries should not be asked by providers to pay for undelivered features.

b. Libraries should not be charged high premiums for essentially development level (beta) products that often do not meet basic client needs.

c. Providers should not expect libraries to pay at present the entire cost of their research and development to bring new electronic products to market. These costs should be shared by the company shareholders and should be amortized by the provider so current prices for electronic information are sufficiently affordable to encourage experimentation and ultimately widespread use. This strategy will offer providers a better long term revenue stream from which to recover their research and development costs.

d. Libraries should have the option to purchase the electronic product without the paper subscription, and the electronic product should cost less than the printed subscription price.

2. Consortia and their member libraries are diverse and have different needs, funding structures, and governance. To meet these differing needs during this current period of experimentation, providers are strongly encouraged to offer multiple and flexible economic models. As libraries and providers gather experience, information, and understanding of the electronic information environment, a richer array of options and solutions should be provided.

3. Bundling electronic and print subscriptions should not be the sole pricing option for purchasing e-information. For example, licenses and purchase agreements for electronic journals should not be premised upon a fixed base year expenditure for purchase of information or contain "no cancellation" clauses that require the library to continue paying for print subscriptions to be able to obtain the electronic version.

C. Access, Archiving, Systems and Licenses.

1. Electronic files (e.g., electronic copies of journal articles) should be available before, or no later than, the publication of the article in its print format. Significant delays in

availability (e.g., of 6 weeks) substantially depreciate the value of electronic publication.

2. The provider should grant to the consortium and its member libraries a perpetual license when the consortium purchases the *content*. That perpetual license must be transferable should the consortium or library wish to change providers, agents or vendors, or to switch from obtaining information from the provider's Web site to local or regional mounting.

   a. Consortia and their member libraries should be allowed to take reasonable steps to archive content that they purchase or lease (e.g., to make backup copies).

   b. When an information provider gives access to data from its Web site (rather than through local mounting of data), the provider should guarantee perpetual availability of the content. This availability need not obligate the provider to realtime access. For example, it may be possible to provide the consortium with copies of data files in an appropriate format, escrowing of data files, or other appropriate means.

3. Consortia or libraries that wish to mount information locally should be allowed the option to do so on the system of their choice. The licensed content should be portable to all major computing platforms and networked environments. All systems and data should comply with appropriate standards as used by libraries (e.g., Z39.50, MARC format). Standard "off-the-shelf" hardware and software solutions are highly preferred to proprietary solutions.

4. Libraries and consortia should have complete flexibility to choose the format in which they wish to receive and store information. Electronic data (bibliographic data, ab-

stracts, and full-text) should be available in multiple formats, e.g., real PDF, HTML, and SGML. The resolution of all images should be at a level appropriate to the material, with at least 600 dpi employed for detailed scientific photographs, data, etc.

5. Licenses should not limit the right of a library or a consortium to integrate the data into local system infrastructures and information services.

D. Content, and Management Data, and Use.

1. Given that e-information provides library clients with the new capabilities and value-added features of the electronic format, providers should not place any undue restrictions or burdens on individual authorized use, such as restrictions on downloading, storing, local printing, use of information for classroom purposes, or electronic reserves.

a. Licenses should permit the "fair use" of all information for non-commercial, educational, instructional, and scientific purposes by authorized users, including unlimited viewing, downloading and printing, in agreement with the provisions in current copyright practices as applicable in the country of origin. Providers should allow e-information (such as electronic copies of journal articles) to be used to generate copies (whether in print or electronic form) for non-commercial interlibrary loans between two academic libraries in support of their teaching, learning and research missions.

b. Libraries should commit to taking reasonable steps to prevent misuse or abuse by clients and to work with the providers as appropriate to stop abuse should it occur. However, license or purchase agreements must not place liability on the licensing/purchasing institution or on consortia for the misuse of content or the product by an individual user. Neither the consortium nor its libraries should be liable for breach of the terms of the agreement by any authorized user as long as the library or consortium did not intentionally assist in or encourage such breach to continue after having received notice by the provider of an actual breach having occurred.

c. Walk-in use by clients who are not formally affiliated with the institution should be included by the provider in the base contract as part of the permitted user group.

2. Agreements with publishers must guarantee individual libraries the right and the opportunity to measure use and to gather the relevant management information needed for collection development. Consortia and their libraries must be allowed to share basic management information about the provider's product. For example, a provider should be willing to generate for every library in a consortium both composite data about the use of the product and itemized statistics of electronic journal use at both the journal title and article level.

3. It is in the best interests of information providers to gather and share data considered by consortia and their libraries to be necessary for consortial and institutional decisionmaking. These data will enhance provider and institutional understanding in the emerging e-information environment.

4. The anonymity of individual users and the confidentiality of their searches must be fully protected.

5. Information providers should not maintain information about individual or institutional use that would violate the other national and international library organization

principles (such as those of the American Library Association) on the ethical use of information or on confidentiality and privacy.

6. In cases where the provider is generating full text files (e.g., electronic journals), MARC bibliographic records for each title should be provided.

E. Authentication.

Information providers should be flexible as to the acceptable mechanisms for authentication or validation of users (e.g., IP addressing, PIN).

ENDNOTES

[1] When this statement was prepared, the adopters were aware of efforts of other groups that might change the underlying structure of the scholarly communication process. For example, the Pew Higher Education Roundtable recently published "To Publish and Perish" in their "Policy Perspectives" series (Philadelphia, PA: Institute for Research on Higher Education, 1998. Available from http://www.irhe.upenn.edu/pp/pp-main.html.

In addition, the American Association of Universities Digital Committee recently circulated an unpublished early draft statement that proposed a possible change to the scholarly communication process by "decoupling" the certification necessary for tenure and promotion from the publication and information dissemination process.

A third relevant development is the work of the ARL Scholarly Publishing & Academic Resources Coalition (SPARC), which seeks to encourage the development of competition in the scholarly publishing marketplace.

[2] While a number of such statements have been developed, in particular we wish to recognize:

- The "Dutch-German Library Joint Licensing Principles and Guidelines" (October 1997), developed by a consortium of universities in the Netherlands and Germany, is available at http://cwis.kub.nl/~dbi/cwis/licprinc.htm

- The "Principles for Licensing Electronic Resources" (July 1997), which was promulgated jointly by the American Association of Law Libraries, the American Library Association, the Association of Academic Health Sciences Libraries, the Association of Research Libraries, the Medical Library Association, and the Special Libraries Association. That statement is available at http://www.arl.org/scomm/licensing/principles.html

- The University of California Libraries Collection Development Committee "Principles for Acquiring and Licensing Information in Digital Formats" (May 1996). Available at http://sunsite.berkeley.edu/Info/principles.html
- The "Basic Principles for Managing Intellectual Property in the Digital Environment from the National Humanities Alliance Committee on Libraries and Intellectual Property Document, which were derived, with permission, from the University of California document. Separately available at http://www-ninch.cni.org/issues/copyright/principles/nha_Complete.html
- Task Force on the CIC Electronic Collection. "Assumptions & Guiding Principles for Near-Term Initiatives." Available at http://NTX2.cso.uiuc.edu/cic/cli/licguide.html

About This Statement

This statement was adopted in principle by member representatives of the "International Coalition of Library Consortia" (ICOLC) whose institutions are listed below. This statement does not necessarily represent the official views of each consortium listed. Consortia listed are in the United States unless otherwise noted.

Adventist Libraries Information Cooperative (ALICE)
AMIGOS Bibliographic Council, Inc.
Arizona Universities Library Consortium (AULC)
Big Twelve Plus Library Consortium
Boston Library Consortium (BLC)
British Columbia Electronic Library Network [Canada]
California Digital Library (CDL)
California State University - Software and Electronic Information Resources (CSU-SEIR)
Center for Digital Information Services (Israel)
Colorado Alliance of Research Libraries
Committee on Institutional Cooperation (CIC) Center for Library Initiatives
Commonwealth Scientific and Industrial Research Organization (CSIRO) [Australia]
Consortium of University Research Libraries (CURL) [United Kingdom]
Council of Australian University Libraries (CAUL) [Australia]

Council of Prairie and Pacific University Libraries (COPPUL)
Florida Center for Library Automation (FCLA) and the
    Florida State University System Library Directors
GALILEO: Georgia Library Learning Online
Gemeinsamer BibliotheksVerbund (GBV) [Germany]
Illinois Cooperative Collection Management Program
Illinois Libraries Computer Sytems Organization (ILCSO)
Louisiana Library Network (LLN)
MINITEX Library Information Network (Minnesota, North
    Dakota, South Dakota)
Missouri Research Consortium of Libraries (MIRACL)
Missouri Research and Education Network (MOREnet)
Netherlands Association of University Libraries, Royal Li-
    brary, and Library of the Royal Academy of Sciences
    (UKB) [Netherlands]
Network of Alabama Academic Libraries (NAAL)
New England Law Library Consortium (NELLCO)
New York Comprehensive Research Libraries (NYCRL)
New Zealand University Librarians, Committee of
NorthEast Research Libraries Consortium (NERL)
OhioLINK
Orbis
Pennsylvania Academic Library Connection Initiative
    (PALCI)
Ontario Academic Research Libraries (OARL) [Canada]
PORTALS
Standing Conference of National and University Libraries
    (SCONUL) [United Kingdom]
TexShare
Triangle Research Libraries Network (TRLN)
University of North Carolina System University Librarians
    Advisory Council
University of Texas System Knowledge Management Center
Virtual Library of Virginia (VIVA)
WALDO
Washington Research Library Consortium (WRLC)
Washington State Cooperative Library Project

About the International Coalition of Library Consortia (ICOLC)

The International Coalition of Library Consortia (ICOLC) is an informal organization that began meeting in 1997. Comprising about sixty library consortia in the United States, Canada, the United Kingdom, the Netherlands, Germany, Israel, and Australia, the Coalition represents over 5,000 member libraries worldwide. The Coalition serves primarily higher education institutions by facilitating discussion among its members on issues of common interest. ICOLC conducts meetings to keep its members informed about new electronic information resources, pricing practices of electronic providers and vendors, and other issues of importance to consortium directors and their governing boards. These meetings also provide a forum for consortial representatives to meet with the information provider community, discuss their products, and engage in a dialog with Coalition members about issues of mutual concern. The ICOLC also maintains listservs and web pages for the benefit of its members. Additional information about the ICOLC can be found at www.library.yale.edu/consortia

Authors of the Statement

* **Arnold Hirshon,** *Vice Provost for Information Resources, Lehigh University*
  8A East Packer Avenue, Bethlehem PA 18015
  Phone: 610/758-3025   Fax: 610/758-3004
  Email: arh5@lehigh.edu
* **Tom Sanville,** *Executive Director, OhioLINK*
  Suite 300, 2455 North Star Road, Columbus, OH 43221
  Phone: 614-728-3600, ext. 322   Fax: 614-728-3610
  Email: tom@ohiolink.edu
* **Ann Okerson,** *Associate University Librarian*
  Yale University, P. O. Box 208240, 130 Wall Street,
  New Haven, CT 06520-8240
  Phone: 203/432-1764   Fax: 203/432-8527
  Email: ann.okerson@yale.edu

- **David Kohl, Dean,** *University Libraries, University of Cincinnati*
  University Libraries, Langsam Library, PO Box 210033, Cincinnati OH 45221
  Phone: 513/556-1515   Fax: 513/556-0325
  Email: david.kohl@uc.edu

International Contacts for the Statement:

In the United Kingdom:
- **Fred Friend,** *Director, Scholarly Communication*
  University College London, Gower Street,
  London England WC1D 6BT
  Phone: 0171-380 7090   Fax: 0171-380 7043
  Email: f.friend@ucl.ac.uk

In Germany:
- **Elmar Mittler,** *Library Director*
  Niedersaechsische Staats- und Universitätsbibliothek Goettingen, Platz der Goettinger Sieben 1,
  37073 Goettingen Germany
  Phone: +49 (551) 39-5212   Fax: +49 (551) 39-5222
  Email: mittler@mail.sub.uni-goettingen.de

In the Netherlands:
- **Hans Geleijnse,** *University Librarian*
  Tilburg University, Katholieke Universiteit Brabant Library, Warandelaan 2, P.O. Box 90153, 5000 LE Tilburg, The Netherlands
  Phone: +31 13 466 21 46   Fax: +31 13 466 33 70
  Email: Geleynse@kub.nl
- **John Gilbert,** *Head Librarian*
  Universiteit Maastricht, P.O Box 616,
  6200 MD Maastricht, The Netherlands
  Phone: +31 43 388 3404   Fax: +31 43 325 6932
  Email: j.gilbert@ub.unimaas.nl

- **Alex Klugkist,** *University Librarian, and Chairman,*
  Dutch University Library Association
  Groningen University, Rijksuniversiteit Groningen,
  Broerstraat 4, Postbus 559,
  9700 AN Groningen, The Netherlands
  Phone: +31 (0)50 363 50 02/3   Fax: +31 (0)50 363 49 96
  Email: a.c.klugkist@ub.rug.nl

For further information on the ICOLC statement see
www.library.yale.edu/consortia/icolcpr.htm.

The authors and the publisher are grateful to Arnold Hirshon
for granting permission to reproduce this statement in its
entirety.

Glossary: Licensing Agreements A–Z

This glossary contains legal terms used in both licensing agreements and copyright law. It not only serves as a ready reference guide to the language of licensing agreements, but it also demonstrates how these terms are interrelated. Terms in capital letters are defined in this chapter.

ACCEPTANCE: one of the three essential components[1] of an ENFORCEABLE CONTRACT or AGREEMENT. For a contract to be enforceable, acceptance of a valid OFFER must be unequivocal and voluntary, and must apply directly to the terms of the offer.[2] Acceptance in a UNILATERAL CONTRACT can be made by the performance of such an act as opening a software carton or clicking on a "yes" button. In a BILATERAL CONTRACT acceptance comes when agreement is reached to the specific terms of an offer.

Acceptance is one of the most troublesome parts of a licensing agreement for libraries and schools. In federal, state, county, municipal, or other publicly supported libraries and schools, statutes or regulations govern who may legally accept an offer or legally sign the contract. In other institutions, a governing body such as a board of trustees of a private university will almost certainly have policies or directives specifying who in that organization is authorized to sign or agree to contracts. In most cases, only the governing board itself can actually accept an offer. Acceptance in all institutions becomes particularly complicated with a SHRINK-WRAP LICENSE. In both public and private institutions employees will be prohibited from agreeing to many of the provisions in such a "take-it-or-leave-it" contract. These and other issues relating to acceptance are discussed fully in Chapter 2. *See also* CONSIDERATION, SIGNATURE AUTHORITY CLAUSE.

ACCORD AND SATISFACTION: an agreement reached between the parties to a contract to accept something less than the strict performance or the full payment as stated under the original contract or agreement.

AD DAMNUM: the amount of damages demanded for BREACH OF CONTRACT (including licensing agreements).[3]

AGREEMENT: a meeting of the minds between parties. For an agreement to be legally enforceable, the parties must exchange mutual promises to do something for some consideration. *See also* ACCEPTANCE, CONSIDERATION, and OFFER.

ALTERNATIVE DISPUTE RESOLUTION CLAUSE: a clause that frequently appears in LICENSING AGREEMENTS. It provides for alternative dispute resolution pathways instead of having to take cases to court. These alternative methods include negotiation, mediation, and arbitration. *See* Chapter 3 for a description of the process, sample language used in this clause, and cautions regarding the use of this method.

AMENDMENTS CLAUSE: many contracts, especially those that are for more than one year, have a clause that allows amendment of the document. *See* Chapter 3 for sample language used in this clause, and cautions regarding its use.

ARTICLE 2B: a new article for the UNIFORM COMMERCIAL CODE, meant to deal with new technology, particularly SHRINK-WRAP LICENSES.

ASSIGNMENT CLAUSE: a clause that frequently appears in LICENSING AGREEMENTS. It (1) prevents the parties from assigning the license to another entity or (2) provides a method for such an assignment. *See* Chapter 3 for sample language used in this clause, and cautions regarding its use.

AUTHORIZED USERS: a term that often appears in LICENSING AGREEMENTS. The term is usually defined in the DEFINITIONS CLAUSE, AUTHORIZED USERS CLAUSE, CONDITIONS OF USE CLAUSE, or SCOPE OF LICENSE CLAUSE in the agreement itself.

AUTHORIZED USERS CLAUSE: a clause that frequently appears in LICENSING AGREEMENTS. It identifies those who may have access to the licensed product and where that access can take place. *See* Chapter 3 for sample language used in this clause, and cautions regarding its use.

BANKRUPTCY: the procedure under Title 11 of the United States Code for discharging a debt. Debts founded on contracts may be dischargeable in bankruptcy, making it particularly important to know the financial status of the OFFEROR(S) or OFFEREE(S) prior to acceptance of a licensing agreement.

BILATERAL CONTRACT: a written agreement that is negotiated and signed by both parties, representing a mutual exchange of promises.

BOILER PLATE: a clause that routinely appears in contracts and is in a standard format. Such a clause is usually not questioned. Caution should be used, therefore, in accepting a clause that is called boiler plate but may be far from routine.

BOXTOP LICENSE: a UNILATERAL contract where notice of the presence of the agreement is found on the top of the packaging but the actual agreement is tucked inside the carton. The agreement inside states that the act of opening the package constituted ACCEPTANCE of the terms and conditions of the agreement even though the user could not possibly have read the agreement before opening the box. *See* Chapter 2 for a discussion of the legality of such licenses, and of the problems they pose.

BREACH OF CONTRACT: failure to perform what is promised in a contract, together with the lack of a legal excuse.[4] A valid excuse for nonperformance of a contract includes IMPOSSIBILITY OF PERFORMANCE.

CAPACITY TO CONTRACT: For an agreement or contract to be legally enforceable, all contracting persons must have the capacity to contract. An individual must, for example, have the legal authority or must be of a legal age for consenting to a contract and must be mentally competent. A corporation must be empowered through its articles of incorporation or charter with the legal capacity to enter into such an agreement.

CLICK-WRAP LICENSE: a UNILATERAL CONTRACT in electronic format that requires the OFFEREE(S) to demonstrate ACCEPTANCE of the terms of a LICENSING AGREEMENT by clicking on a "yes" button just before or following the full text of the agreement. A "yes" response is usually required before the software or database may be fully accessed or used. A "no" response locks the user out. These agreements contrast with SHRINK-WRAP

LICENSES where a user may not have access to the text of the licensing agreement before having to agree to it. *See* Chapter 2 for discussion of the legality of such licenses, and of the problems they posed.

COMPLETE AGREEMENT CLAUSE: a clause, based on the PAROL EVIDENCE RULE, that frequently appears in LICENSING AGREEMENTS. It generally states that "This Agreement with its attachments comprises the entire agreement between the parties with respect to its subject matter. It supersedes any and all previous agreements oral or written between the parties." From the OFFEROR's point of view this clause ensures that all terms of the agreement are understood. From the offeree's position this clause means that the final written agreement is comprehensive.

CONDITIONS OF USE CLAUSE: a clause that frequently appears in LICENSING AGREEMENTS. It deals with identification of the uses and users to which the OFFEREE is entitled. The phrase "AUTHORIZED USERS" often appears in this clause. In libraries and schools, uses are generally limited to personal and noncommercial categories. *See* Chapter 3 for sample language used in this clause, and cautions regarding its interpretation.

CONFIDENTIALITY CLAUSE: a clause that frequently appears in LICENSING AGREEMENTS. It represents the OFFEROR's attempt to keep confidential some of the terms of the agreement between the parties. This kind of clause hinders OFFEREES who are interested in sharing information about the contracting process. *See* Chapter 3 for sample language used in this clause, and cautions regarding its interpretation.

CONSIDERATION: one of the three essential components[5] of an ENFORCEABLE CONTRACT or agreement. Consideration may be money or some other inducement for fulfilling the contract. In some cases, a promise for a promise may be adequate consideration.[6] *See also* OFFER, ACCEPTANCE.

CONTENT AND COPYRIGHT CLAUSE: a clause that appears less frequently in LICENSING AGREEMENTS. It requires the OFFEREE to acknowledge that the OFFEROR holds the rights to the copyright and trade secrets involved with the leased materials. One variation of this clause requires that the offeree exercise reasonable care in protecting the offeror's copyright and trade secrets. Part of this duty requires prevention of unauthorized use or copying of the licensed product. *See* Chapter 3 for sample language used in this clause, and cautions regarding its interpretation.

CONTRACT: a legally enforceable agreement between two or more people, agencies, companies, institutions, or other entities (called "parties to the contract") that involves an exchange of mutual promises to do something for some CONSIDERATION. See also ACCEPTANCE, OFFER.

DAMAGES: a possible remedy for BREACH OF CONTRACT, requiring money payment.

DEFINITIONS CLAUSE: a clause that frequently appears in LICENSING AGREEMENTS. It contains definitions of important terms included in the body of the license. *See* Chapter 3 for sample language used in this clause, and cautions regarding its use.

DISCHARGE OF A CONTRACT: the end or termination of legal duties of one of the parties. Some of the means of discharging a contract are complete performance, ACCORD AND SATISFACTION, and RESCISSION.

DISCLAIMER CLAUSE: *see* LIMITATION OF LIABILITY CLAUSE.

DOCUMENTATION CLAUSE: *see* SUPPORT CLAUSE.

ENFORCEABLE CONTRACT: in order for a contract or agreement to be valid and enforceable in court, there must be an OFFER, an ACCEPTANCE, and CONSIDERATION. In addition, the terms of the agreement—whether written, oral, or implied—must be specific enough to determine the obligations of each party.[7]

ENTIRE AGREEMENT CLAUSE: *See* COMPLETE AGREEMENT CLAUSE.

EULA: end user license agreement. A eula is a form of SHRINK-WRAP LICENSE.

FACTS AND IDEAS EXCEPTION: the doctrine that facts and ideas cannot be copyrighted.

FAIR USE: the doctrine that allows the use of portions of copyrighted materials without first securing permission of the copyright owner or paying any licensing fee.[8]

FEES CLAUSE: a clause that frequently appears in LICENSING AGREEMENTS. It deals with how the OFFEREE will be billed for use. This is one of the most important clauses for both the OFFEROR and OFFEREE. *See* Chapter 3 for a listing of the advantages and disadvantages of the four broad payment methods, as well as a list of the factors that have an impact on the pricing of information products.

FIRST SALE DOCTRINE: the doctrine that allows the resale or loan of a copy of a copyrighted work after it is first sold, without payment of an additional fee to the copyright holder. This doctrine is at the heart of such library activities as circulation and Friends of the Library book sales.

FORCE MAJEURE CLAUSE: a clause that appears less frequently in LICENSING AGREEMENTS. It protects the nonperforming party from liability if some outside major force (such as the outbreak of war, an Act of God, or even a failure brought about by a subcontractor), results in the IMPOSSIBILITY OF PERFORMANCE. *See* Chapter 3 for sample language used in this clause, and cautions regarding its use.

FORUM: the law of the state that will govern whether a CONTRACT is valid and how it will be interpreted and enforced.[9] This designation is usually stated in the GOVERNING LAW CLAUSE.

FRAUD: intentional deception used by one party to induce the other party to contract. A VOIDABLE CONTRACT results.

GOVERNING LAW CLAUSE: a clause that frequently appears in LICENSING AGREEMENTS. It takes the form: "This Agreement will be governed by the laws of the state of New York." While this clause seems harmless, its implications are not. *See* Chapter 3 for cautions in the use of this clause.

GOVERNMENT USE CLAUSE: a clause that appears in a LICENSING AGREEMENT when the OFFEREE is acting for a unit or agency of the United States government. Because special provisions apply and can change from time to time, those who are in such a situation should check carefully with their agency head to ensure compliance with the procedures and rules in effect for the licensing period.

GRANT CLAUSE: a clause that frequently appears in LICENSING AGREEMENTS. It states, in general terms, what the OFFEROR is providing to the OFFEREE. *See*

Chapter 3 for sample language used in this clause, and cautions regarding its use.

HOLD HARMLESS CLAUSE: *See* INDEMNIFICATION CLAUSE

IMPOSSIBILITY OF PERFORMANCE: defense to non-performance of a contract, based on unforeseen and extreme circumstances, such as death of one of the parties or irretrievable loss or destruction of a product. *See also* FORCE MAJEURE CLAUSE.

INDEMNIFICATION CLAUSE: a clause that appears less frequently in LICENSING AGREEMENTS. It generally takes the form: "Licensee agrees to indemnify Zychon and to hold Zychon harmless from any and all claims of third parties that may arise relating to licensee's use of the licensed materials, regardless of whether such claims were foreseeable by the licensor." This clause insulates the OFFEROR from all claims, and burdens the OFFEREE with responsibility should something go wrong. This type of clause should not be agreed to. *See* Chapter 3 for further discussion.

INTEGRATION CLAUSE: *See* COMPLETE AGREEMENT CLAUSE.

LAW GOVERNING DISPUTE CLAUSE: *See* GOVERNING LAW CLAUSE.

LEGAL AGE: the minimum age established by state law for legally consenting to a CONTRACT.

LEX LOCI CONTRACTUS: literally, the place of making a contract. It is important because the law governing a contract or licensing agreement is the state (place) in which the agreement is signed. Sometimes licensing agreements have a clause stating that the law governing the contract is another state. In such cases, the law of the state designated in the licensing agreement, not the *lex loci contractus* where the contract was signed, governs.

LICENSEE: the party accepting an offer.

LICENSING AGREEMENT: a form of CONTRACT; sometimes called a license.

LICENSOR: the party making an offer.

LICENSOR OBLIGATIONS CLAUSE: a clause that frequently appears in LICENSING AGREEMENTS. It specifies what the OFFEREE can expect from the OFFEROR. This clause may also state that a reasonable effort will be made by the offeror to have the system function as well as other similar systems. *See* Chapter 3 for sample language used in this clause, and cautions regarding its use.

LIMITATION OF LIABILITY CLAUSE: a clause that frequently appears in LICENSING AGREEMENTS. In this clause the OFFEROR will deny any responsibility for errors or defects in the product being licensed. *See* Chapter 3 for sample language used in this clause, and cautions regarding its use. For example, in one such clause an OFFEROR while disclaiming any liability at all, has at the same time noted a limitation of liability of no more than the fee paid—thus covering all the bases.

MISTAKE: an omission resulting from a misconception or lack of information. A mistake could result in the RESCISSION of a contract.

MONITORING USE CLAUSE: a clause that appears less frequently in LICENSING AGREEMENTS. It asks or requires the OFFEREE to provide usage statistics to the

OFFEROR. *See* Chapter 3 for sample language used in this clause, and a discussion of the advantages and disadvantages of supplying this information.

NEGOTIATED-CLAUSE-BY-CLAUSE CONTRACT: a BILATERAL contract for which the language of each and every clause results from a give-and-take conversation and ultimately represents a mutual agreement. Also called a negotiated contract.

NOVATION: a change in the parties to a contract in which, with the mutual agreement of all the parties, one of the original parties removes himself or herself from the contract and is replaced by a newcomer. The agreement is then between the remaining original party and the newcomer.

OFFER: one of the three essential components[10] of an enforceable contract or agreement. An offer demonstrates a willingness to enter into a bargain and is a visible signal to the other party that the deal offered would now be welcome. As with the other two essential components—ACCEPTANCE and CONSIDERATION—it is crucial that the offer be specific enough to define the terms of the resulting agreement.[11]

OFFEREE(S): the party or parties accepting an offer.

OFFEROR(S): the party or parties making an offer.

ORAL CONTRACT: a nonwritten CONTRACT, or a written contract that has not been signed by both parties.

PAROL EVIDENCE RULE: one of the most significant rules in contract interpretation for LICENSING AGREEMENTS. The rule states that when a licensing agreement is put into writing in its final form, oral (*parol*) evidence of earlier agreements is not admissible. In short, no matter what promises are made to the OFFEREE(S) by sales or customer representatives, if these promises are not included in the final written licensing agreement they are not relevant in interpreting a contract. This rule is usually stated in the COMPLETE AGREEMENT CLAUSE of a licensing agreement.

PARTIES CLAUSE: usually the first clause, identifying the parties, in a LICENSING AGREEMENT. It is very important that both OFFEROR and OFFEREE be properly identified, either in this clause or somewhere else in the licensing agreement.

PARTIES TO A CONTRACT: persons or institutions making the offer (OFFEROR) and those accepting the offer (OFFEREE).

PRIVACY PROTECTION: a clause that appears less frequently in LICENSING AGREEMENTS is one in which the OFFEROR seeks detailed information about searchers and searches. There could even be a request for the name(s) of users, their status, and/or the specific information they sought. *This clause must be struck from a license or carefully modified to avoid improper invasion of user privacy.* Often there will be no such clause.

ProCD CASE: a case[12] appealed and later reversed by the Seventh Circuit Federal Court of Appeals in 1966. The case, which deals with SHRINK-WRAP LICENSES, played a significant role in the development of ARTICLE 2B of the UNIFORM COMMERCIAL CODE. *See* Chapter 2 for further detail.

REFORMATION OF A CONTRACT: redrafting of a contract because the contract as written does not express the true wishes of both parties.

REMEDIES FOR BREACH OF CONTRACT: the legal or equitable remedies available to a party aggrieved by the failure of another to fulfill their obligations under a contract. Remedies can include DAMAGES or SPECIFIC PERFORMANCE.

RENEWAL CLAUSE: a clause, dealing with procedures for renewal, that frequently appears in LICENSING AGREE-MENTS. *See* Chapter 3 for sample language used in this clause, and cautions about complying with its various versions.

RESCISSION: cancellation of a contract, usually by mutual agreement.

SATISFACTION: *See* ACCORD AND SATISFACTION.

SCOPE OF LICENSE CLAUSE: *See* CONDITIONS OF USE CLAUSE.

SEVERABILITY CLAUSE: a clause that frequently appears in LICENSING AGREEMENTS. It protects the remainder of the agreement if some part of the license is found to be invalid or unenforceable. Usually it states: "If any part of this Agreement is found to be unenforceable or invalid, that part shall be set apart and the rest of the Agreement shall continue in effect." This clause is usually BOILER PLATE.

SHRINK-WRAP LICENSE: a UNILATERAL agreement usually found tucked in the packaging of computer software, and stating that opening of the software package constitutes acceptance of the terms and conditions in the agreement. The user is sometimes not given the opportunity to read the licensing agreement in its entirety before opening the box. *See* Chapter 2 for a review of court cases dealing with the legality of shrink-wrap licenses, and a discussion of the particular problems that such licenses pose.

SIGNATURE AUTHORITY CLAUSE: a clause that appears less frequently in LICENSING AGREEMENTS. It seeks a guarantee that the person who signs for a party has the authority to do so. *See* Chapter 3 for sample language used in this clause, and cautions regarding its use.

SPECIFIC PERFORMANCE: a possible remedy for breach of contract, requiring complete performance of the contract as agreed to.

STATUTE OF FRAUDS: law in most states, requiring that certain types of contracts be in writing to be valid.

SUBSTITUTE CONTRACT: a contract that discharges an earlier contract, drawn up when the parties agree to a different performance or performer for the promises stipulated in the original contract.

SUPPORT CLAUSE: a clause that frequently appears in LICENSING AGREEMENTS. It describes generally or in detail the support that the OFFEREE can expect from the OFFEROR. *See* Chapter 3 for sample language used in this clause, and cautions regarding its use.

TEAR-OPEN LICENSE: a UNILATERAL CONTRACT where notice of the presence of the agreement is found on the packaging but the actual agreement is tucked inside the carton. The agreement inside states that the act of opening the package constituted ACCEPTANCE of the terms and conditions of the agreement even though the user could not possibly have read the agreement before opening the box. *See* Chapter 2 for a discussion of the legality of such licenses, and of the problems they pose.

TERM CLAUSE: a clause that frequently appears in LICENSING AGREEMENTS. It states how long the agreement runs and may state how the license can be renewed. A term clause states both the term and conditions for renewal. *See* Chapter 3 for sample language used in this clause, and cautions regarding its use.

TERMINATION CLAUSE: a clause that frequently appears in LICENSING AGREEMENTS. It provides a way for each of the parties, with proper notice, to terminate the agreement. There are usually two parts to the notice requirement—that it be in writing and that it be given within a specified time. *See* Chapter 3 for sample language used in this clause, and cautions regarding its use.

ULTRA VIRES: literally, outside its powers. If a company contracts to do something that it is not empowered by its articles of incorporation or its charter to do, it acts *ultra vires*. Such a contract is VOIDABLE and may be judged unenforceable. *See also* CAPACITY TO CONTRACT.

UNIFORM COMMERCIAL CODE (UCC): the law governing commercial transactions. The UCC was originally drafted by the National Conference of Commissioners on Uniform State Laws but it has since been adopted in whole or in part by all state legislatures. Proposed ARTICLE 2B of the UCC deals with SHRINK-WRAP LICENSES.

UNILATERAL CONTRACT: a one-sided agreement, such as a SHRINK-WRAP LICENSE, where the vendor (OFFEROR) gains the user's (OFFEREE'S) ACCEPTANCE when the user performs an act such as opening a software carton. Such a contract is in contrast to a BILATERAL CONTRACT, where there is a mutual exchange of promises.

VOIDABLE CONTRACT: a contract, such as one induced through fraud or misrepresentation, that has the potential to be voided. Such a contract is not automatically void; it will stand unless an aggrieved party requests that the contract be voided.

WAIVER CLAUSE: a clause that frequently appears in LICENSING AGREEMENTS. It prevents the simple failure to enforce a provision of the agreement from constituting a waiver. In short, ignoring a BREACH OF CONTRACT does not endorse the breach.

WEBWRAP LICENSE: a UNILATERAL CONTRACT found on the Internet that requires the OFFEREE(S) to demonstrate ACCEPTANCE of the terms of a LICENSING AGREEMENT by clicking on a "yes" button just before or following the full text of the agreement. A "yes" response is usually required before the Web site may be fully used. A "no" response prevents the user from entering the site or obtaining access to some information on it. *See* Chapter 2 for a discussion of the legality of such licenses, and of the problems they pose.

NOTES

1. "For an enforceable contract to exist, there must be an offer, an acceptance, consideration, and sufficient specification of terms so that obligations involved can be ascertained." *Savoca Masonry Co., Inc. v. Homes and Son Construction Company, Inc.*, 112 Ariz. 392, 542 P.2d 817 (1975).
2. *K-Line Builders, Inc. v. First Federal Savings & Loan Association*, 677 P.2d 1317, 1320 (1983).
3. *Cole v. Hayes*, 7 A. 391, 392 (1886).
4. *Realty Development Co., Inc. v. Wakefield Ready-Mixed Concrete Co., Inc.*, 100 N.E.2d 28 at 30 (Mass. 1951).
5. *Savoca Masonry Co., Inc. v. Homes and Son Construction Company, Inc.*, 112 Ariz. 392, 542 P.2d 817 (1975).
6. *Tucson Federal Savings & Loan Association v. Aetna Investment Corporation*, 74 Ariz. 163, 245 P.2d 423 (1940).
7. *Savoca Masonry Co., Inc. v. Homes and Son Construction Company, Inc.*, 112 Ariz. 392, 542 P.2d 817 (1975).
8. *See* 17 USC §107.

9. *Rubin v. Gallagher*, 292 N.W. 584 at 586 (Mich. 1940).
10. *Savoca Masonry Co., Inc. v. Homes and Son Construction Company, Inc.*, 112 Ariz. 392, 542 P.2d 817 (1975).
11. See *Restatement of the Law of Contracts 2d* §24.
12. *ProCD, Inc. v. Zeidenberg*, 908 F. Supp. 640 (1966), rev'd 86 F.3d 1447(1966).

Index

A

Acceptance, definition, 137–138
Access phone lines, 53
Accord and satisfaction, 12
  definition, 138
Account stated, 12–13
Act of God, 80
Ad damnum, definition, 138
Agreement, definition, 138
Alternative Dispute Resolution
  Clause, 61, 62–64
  definition, 138
Amendments Clause, 79
  definition, 138
American Arbitration Association (AAA), 64
Arbitration, 61, 62–64
Archives, special rights under
  copyright law, 93
*Arizonia Retail Systems, Inc, v.
  the Software Link, Inc.*
  (1993), 19–20
Article 2B, UCC, 10, 20
  definition, 139
"As is," 56
Assignment Clause, 68
  definition, 139
Association libraries, 6, 17, 21–22, 58

B

Authorized Users Clause, 54–55
  definition, 139

Bankruptcy, 4–5, 13, 139
Bid process, 6, 7
Bilateral contracts, 3, 10, 11
  definition, 139
Block access charge, 50
Bobbs-Merrill, Co. v. Strauss
  (1908), 88
Boiler plate, 70
  definition,139
Box top license, definition, 140
Branch libraries, 55
Breach of contract, 13–14
  defenses to, 14–15
  definition, 140
  effect of ignoring, 69
  endorsement of, 69

C

Cancellation, 42, 58–59
Capacity to contract, 4–7, 81
  definition, 140
Carriers, 80
Charges, block access, 49
Charges,
  per search, 49

subscription, 49
timed access, 49
Checklist, 107–111
Click-wrap licenses, 17, 22–23
   definition, 140
Colleges libraries and schools,
   7, 17, 34, 47, 54, 56, 68,
   81
   shrink-wrap licenses, 99
Competency (legal) to contract,
   4–7, 81
Complete Agreement Clause,
   65
   definition, 141
Computer programs, lending,
   89
Computer Software Rental
   Amendments, Act of
   1989, 18
Conditions of Use Clause, 51–
   53
   definition, 141
Confidentiality Clause, 71
   definition, 141
Consent of all parties, 44
Consideration, definition, 141–
   142
Content and Copyright Clause,
   73
   definition, 142
Contract year, 58
Contract, competency to make,
   4–7, 81
Contracts, basics of , 3–15
Contracts, bilateral, 3, 10, 11
   definition,139
Contracts
   definition, 142
   elements of, 5
   enforceable, 4
   enforcement, oral, 8–9
   express, 8
   governed by state law, 60–61
   illegality, 15

implied, 3
law governing, 60–61, 62
oral, 3, 7–8
rescission, 11–12
substitute, 12
unenforceable, 3, 4, 14
unilateral, 3, 10, 18
voidable, 3, 4, 14
   definition, 151–152
written, 3, 7–10
Conversion costs, 47
Copying license materials,
   limitation on, 73
Copyright Clause of the Constitution, 71, 88
Copyright, rights under, 85–94
Corporations, 5–6, 17, 21–22
Counties, 6, 17, 21–22
Court cases, 85

D
Damages, definition, 142
Dates, 40–41
Defects, 56
Defenses, breach of contract,
   14–15
Definitions Clause, 33–34
   cautions, 34
   definition, 142
Digital Millennium Copyright
   Act of 1998, 93–94
   text, 113–117
Discharge of a contract, 11–12
   definition, 142
Disclaimer Clause, 56–57
   definition, 142
Documentation Clause, 66–67
   definition, 143
Download statistics, 74
Downtime, 38, 80
Due notice, 43
Duress, 14

E
Enforceable contract, 4
  definition, 143
Enforcement, failure, 69
Entire Agreement Clause, 65
  definition, 143
Equipment supplied, 53
EULA (end user license agree-
  ment), 17
EULA (end user license agree-
  ment), definition, 143
Exhibitions, 89

F
Facts and ideas exception, 86–
  88
  definition, 143
Failure of consideration, 15
Fair pricing, 47–48
Fair use (copyright law), 25,
  91–93
  definition, 143
FAQ support, 67
Fees Clause, 46, 47–50
  definition, 143
Fees, 47–48, 54
Fires, 80
First sale doctrine, 24, 88–91
  definition, 143
Fiscal year, 58
Floods, 80
Force Majeure Clause, 34, 80
  definition, 144
Forum, definition, 144
Fraud, definition, 144
Friends of the Library, 86
Future pricing-structure, 47

G
Governing Law Clause, 60–61
  definition, 144
Government reports, 85
Government Use Clause, 78
  definition, 144

Grant Clause, 35–36
  definition, 144–145

H
*Harrison v. Maynard, Merrill
  & Co.* (1884), 88
Hold Harmless Clause, 77
  definition, 145

I
*ICOLC Statement of Current
  Prospective and Preferred
  Practices for the Selection
  and Purchase of Elec-
  tronic Information*, 119–
  136
Illegal contract, 15
Illegal provision in a contract,
  70
Impossibility of performance,
  definition, 145
Incompetent party, 5,6, 81
Indemnification or Hold Harm-
  less Clause, 77
  definition, 145
Interlibrary loans, 47
International Coalition of
  Library Consortia
  (ICOLC), 119–136
Internet licenses, 17, 22–23
Internet servers, delays caused
  by, 38
Intranets, 17, 22–23
Invalid provision, 70
Invasion of privacy, 76

L
Law governing, 60–61, 62
Legal age, definition, 145
Legislative proceedings, 85
Lex loci contractus, definition,
  145–146
Liability of provider, 56–57
Libraries and Library Boards,

5, 6, 17, 21–22, 58
rights under copyright law, 86
Libraries, special rights under copyright law, 93
Licensee, definition, 146
Licensing agreements,
as written contracts, 10
checklist, 107
definition, 3, 146
prevalence, 24–25
types, 17
Licensor Obligations Clause, 37–38
definition, 146
Licensor, definition, 146
Limitation of Liability Clause, 56–57
definition, 146

M
Macy, R.H., & Company, 88–89
Mediation, 61, 62–64
Mental capacity to contract, 14
Method of payment,
block access, 50
per search, 50
subscription, 49
timed access, 49
Misrepresentation, 14
Mistake, 14
definition, 146
Modems, 53
Modifications of agreements, 79
Monitoring Use Clause, 74–75
definition, 146–147
Multi-year agreement, 58
Municipalities, 6, 7, 17, 34, 47, 54, 56, 68, 81

N
Negotiated clause-by-clause contract, definition, 147

Negotiated clause-by-clause licenses, 17
Negotiated licenses, 17, 23–24
Negotiation (process), 63, 99–105
banding together, 105
how to, 102–104
Newsletters provided, 67
Nonexclusive right to access, 36
Nontransferable right to access, 36
Notice of intention, 46, 58
Novation, 12
definition, 147

O
Offer, definition, 147
Offeree(s), definition, 147
Offeror(s), definition, 147
On-site access, 52
Oral Contract, definition, 147

P
Parol evidence rule, definition, 147–148
Parties to the Contract Clause, 32
definition, 148
Parties to the contract, 3, 5, 32, 81,
definition, 148
Payment schedule changes, 43
Payment schedule, 47–48
Per search charge, 50
Permission to use without fee, 85
Personal, noncommercial use, 52
Phonorecords, lending, 89
Privacy Protection Clause, 76
definition, 148
Private colleges, 6, 17
ProCD case, definition, 148

ProCD, Inc, v. Zeidenberg, (1996), 19–21
Proper notice, 58

R
Reasonable care standard, 73
Reasonable effort, 38
Reasonable support, 66
Rebates, 58–59
Reformation of a contract, 148
Refunds, 58–59
Remedies, breach of contract, 13–14
  definition, 149
Remedies, specific performance, 13–14
Remote access, 54–55
Renewal Clause, 42–46
  automatic renewal, 42–43
  definition, 151
  nonautomatic renewal, 42, 44
Reporting requirements, 74–75
Rescission
  definition, 149
  of a contract, 11–12
Research facilities, 4–7, 34, 47, 55, 56, 81, 99
Reverse engineering, 52

S
School libraries or systems, 7, 17, 21–22, 34, 47, 54, 56, 61, 68, 81, 99
  duration of contract, 58
  rights under copyright, 86
  shrink-wrap licenses, 99
School year, 58
Scope of License Clause, 51–53
Section 108 (copyright law), 93
Severability Clause, 70
  definition, 149
Shrink-wrap contracts, 10–11, 17–22, 99
  definition, 149–150

Signature Authority Clause, 81
  definition, 150
Signing agreement, 4–7, 81
Similar systems (performance), 38
Site restrictions, 52
Source codes, 52
Specific performance, 13–14
  definition, 150
State institutions, 7, 17, 34, 47, 54, 56, 68, 81
State laws, which applies?, 60–61
Statistics reporting, 74
Statute of Frauds, 9
  definition, 150
Step-Saver Data Systems, Inc. v. Wyse Technology and the Software Link, Inc. (1991), 19–20
Subcontractor, 80
Subscription charge, 49
Substitute contract, 12, 150
Superintendent of schools, 5, 17, 21–22, 81
Suppliers, 80
Support Clause, 66–67
  definition, 150

T
Tear-open license, definition, 150
Technical support provisions, 66–67
Telephone equipment, 53
Term and Renewal Clause, 39–41, 45–46
Term Clause, 39–41
  definition, 151
Termination Clause, 58–59
  definition, 151
Terms of license, confidentiality, 71
Timed access charge, 49

Toll-free phone numbers, 67
Training, 47

U

Ultra vires, 5
  definition, 151
Unenforceable provision, 70
Uniform Commercial Code, 4,
  9–10, 20
  definition, 151
Unilateral contracts, 3, 10, 18
  definition, 151
Universities libraries and
  schools, 7, 17, 34, 47, 54,
  56, 68, 81
Universities, 6, 17, 21–22, 26,
  99

V

Vault Corp. v. Quaid Software,
Ltd. (1988), 19–20
Voidable contract, definition,
  151–152

W

Waiver Clause, 69
  definition, 152
Warning of Copyright for
  Software Lending by
  Nonprofit Libraries, 90
Warrantees, 56
Websites, negotiation process,
  100–101
Webwrap licenses, 17, 22–23,
  99
  definition, 152

Y

Year (calendar, fiscal, or
  contract?), 58

About the Authors

Arlene Bielefield is on the faculty of the Department of Library Science and Instructional Technology at Southern Connecticut State University (SCSU) in New Haven, Connecticut. Arlene holds a Juris Doctor from the University of Connecticut School of Law and passed the Connecticut Bar in 1981. She also holds a Masters in Library Science degree from SCSU.

In 1994, Arlene authored *Legally Effective Corporate Communication* for Panel Books. A past president of the Connecticut Library Association (CLA), Arlene has served on a number of professional committees. She has won both the CLA Connecticut Librarian of the Year Award and the Distinguished Alumna award from the library school. She is increasingly in demand as a speaker on copyright.

Lawrence Cheeseman holds a Master's in Library and Information Science degree from Pratt Institute and has been a practicing law librarian for over 30 years. He currently supervises a group of seven public law libraries. A past president of the Southern New England Association of Law Librarians, he now serves as the chair of their Publication Committee.

In 1992, Arlene and Larry wrote the *Connecticut Legal Research Handbook* for the Connecticut Law Book Company.

In 1993, they wrote their first copyright book, *Libraries and Copyright Law,* the introductory volume in the Libraries and the Law Series for Neal-Schuman Publishers. This was followed by *Library Employment and the Law* (1993), *Maintaining the Privacy of Library Records* (1994), *Library Patrons and the Law* (1995), and *Technology and Copyright Law: A Guidebook for the Library, Research, and Teaching Professions,* (1997), which was selected by *Library Journal* for inclusion in its First Annual List of Best Professional Reading (1998).